GW01607183

SKY HIGH

SUSSEX

AN AERIAL JOURNEY

SKYWORKS

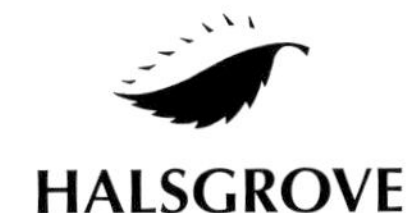

HALSGROVE

First published in Great Britain in 2007

British Library Cataloguing-in-Publication Data
A CIP record for this title is available from the British Library

ISBN 978 1 84114 686 7

HALSGROVE
Halsgrove House
Ryelands Industrial Estate
Bagley Road, Wellington
Somerset TA21 9PZ
Tel: 01823 653777
Fax: 01823 216796
email: sales@halsgrove.com
website: www.halsgrove.com

Printed and bound by Grafiche Flaminia, Italy

Introduction

'Sussex by the Sea' is how this most famous part of England is popularly known and it is true that the presence of the sea has had an enormous impact on it from ancient times to the present day. The Romans came by sea to settle the area, and the most well-known sea-borne invasion in English history took place at Hastings in 1066 when William of Normandy defeated the native Harold and his Saxon armies, an event the Conqueror celebrated by building Battle Abbey. In the eighteenth century a new trend set in as sea-water bathing became fashionable and – with easy access from London – the stylish flocked to the Sussex coast. Brighton became easily the most famous resort, but with the coming of the railways others – including Eastbourne – grew rapidly too and are today amongst some of the most famous holiday haunts in Britain.

Inland, the pace of life was slower. Sussex has still very much a farmed and pastoral countryside and the Downs, the rolling chalkland that extends for some 90km from Eastbourne to the Hampshire border, are planned to become the first National Park in South East England.

Sussex can boast an impressive number of picturesque villages and small towns. Its climate and soils have made it particularly suitable for the creation of gardens and parks which accompany the country houses for which Sussex is legendary. Almost everywhere you look there is a trace of its rich past in its thriving present, and – particularly when seen from above in this aerial journey – an incomparable variety of wood and field, down and village, framed by one of the most renowned coastlines in the world.

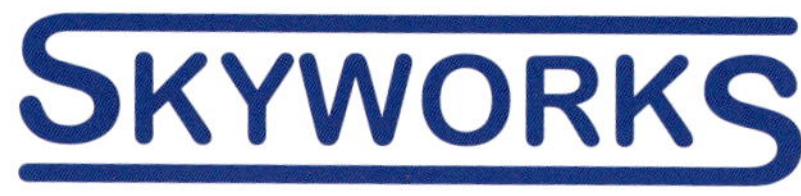

For aerial shots with impact, look no further...

Skyworks is an independent television production company and a stock footage library specialising in top-end High Definition filming from the air. The company has become one of the world's leading HD aerial archives for High Definition video and stills.

On the television side, Skyworks produces a range of factual programmes, varying from series about history, landscape and heritage to observational documentaries and more recently drama-documentary. Skyworks has produced over 100 factual programmes for international broadcasters, including the BBC, Discovery and ITV.

The Skyworks' team is systematically travelling the globe and filming locations in the unique style for which the company has become renowned. Skyworks' archive collection is already geographically broad and thematically diverse. The company's vision is to continue filming until the world has been covered and catalogued for all to see.

www.skyworks.co.uk

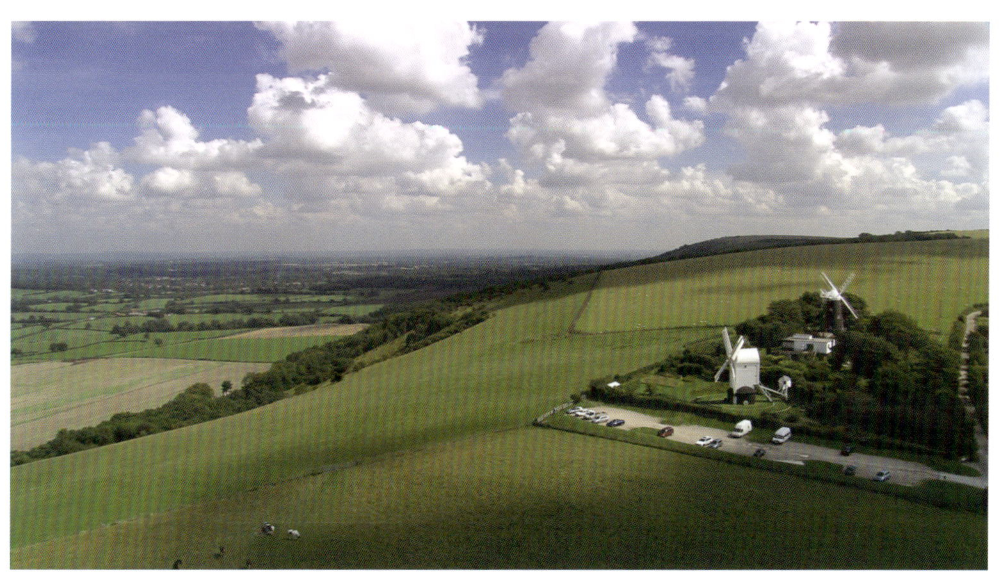

The Sussex Downs. Rudyard Kipling, who lived in Sussex, called them the 'blunt, bow-headed, whale-backed downs.'

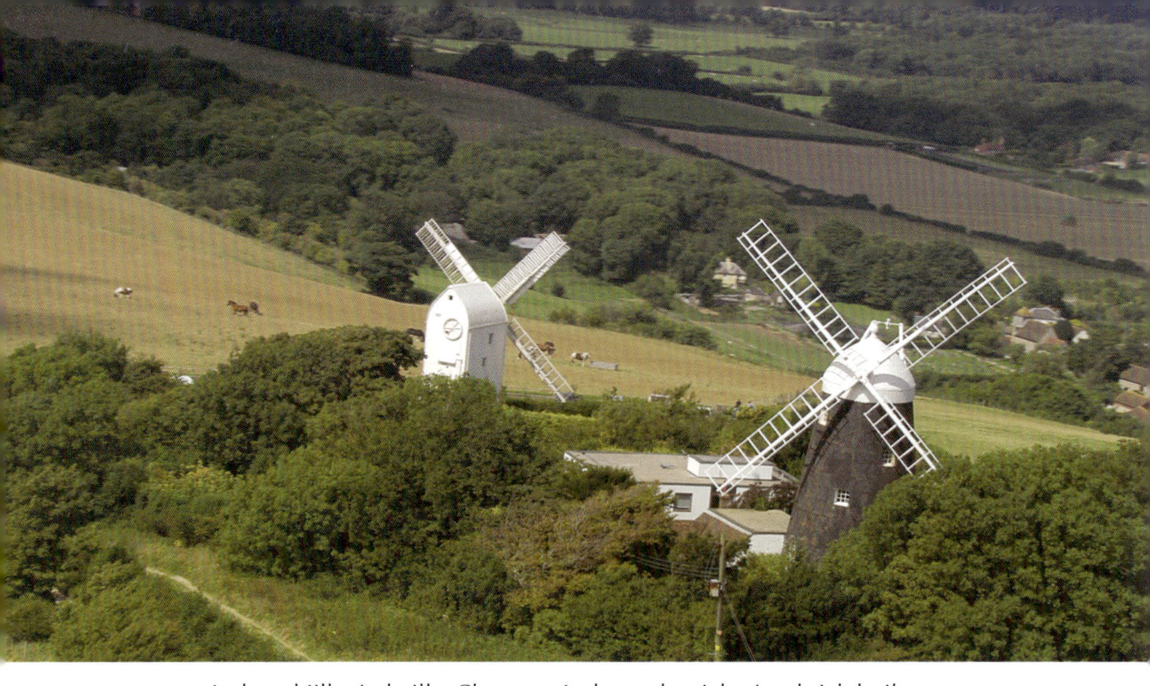

Jack and Jill windmills, Clayton. Jack, on the right, is a brick-built tower mill of the 1890s; Jill, on the left, is a timber post mill of about 1820.

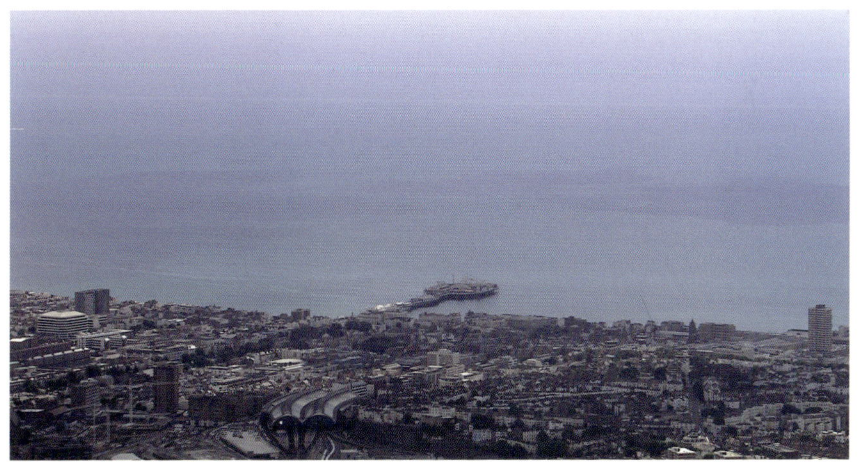

Brighton. The coming of the railways (centre foreground) in 1841 turned Brighton from a genteel watering place to a rapidly-expanding tourist centre.

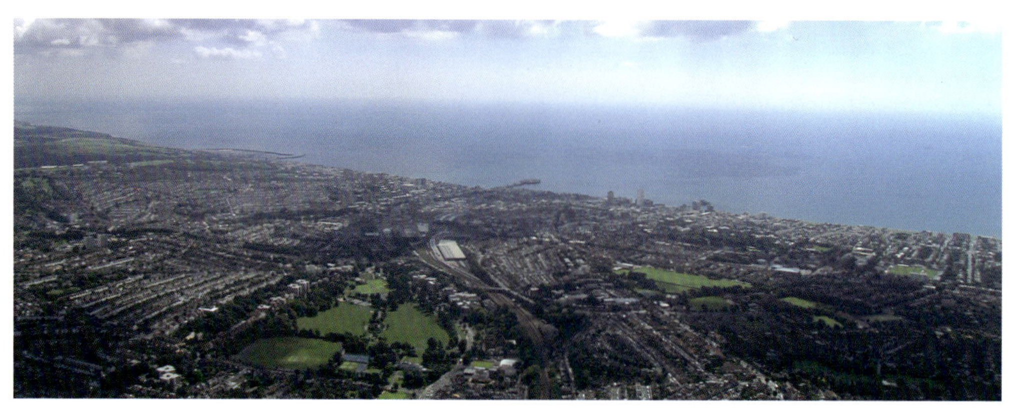

Brighton. Originally a small fishing village, Brighton began to prosper in the late 1700s, when sea-bathing became fashionable.

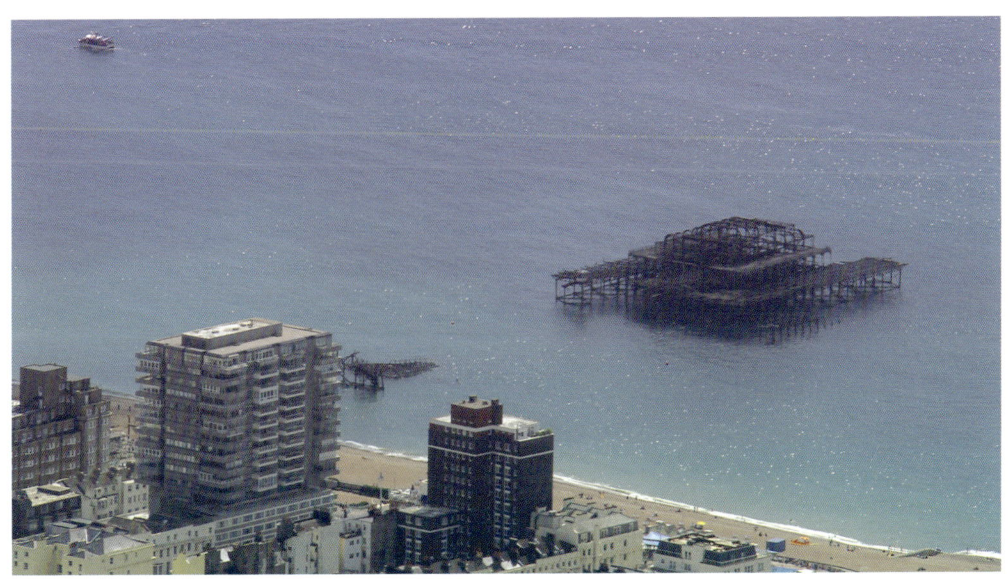

Brighton. Old and new as tower blocks look out on the fire-ravaged skeleton of the West Pier.

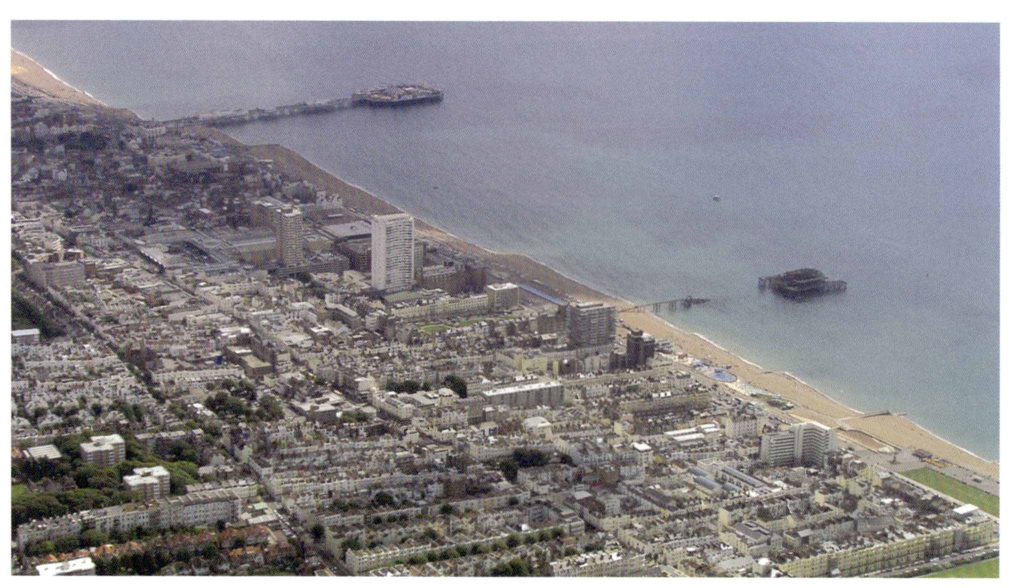

Brighton. The two piers – the West Pier on the right and Brighton Pier on the left.

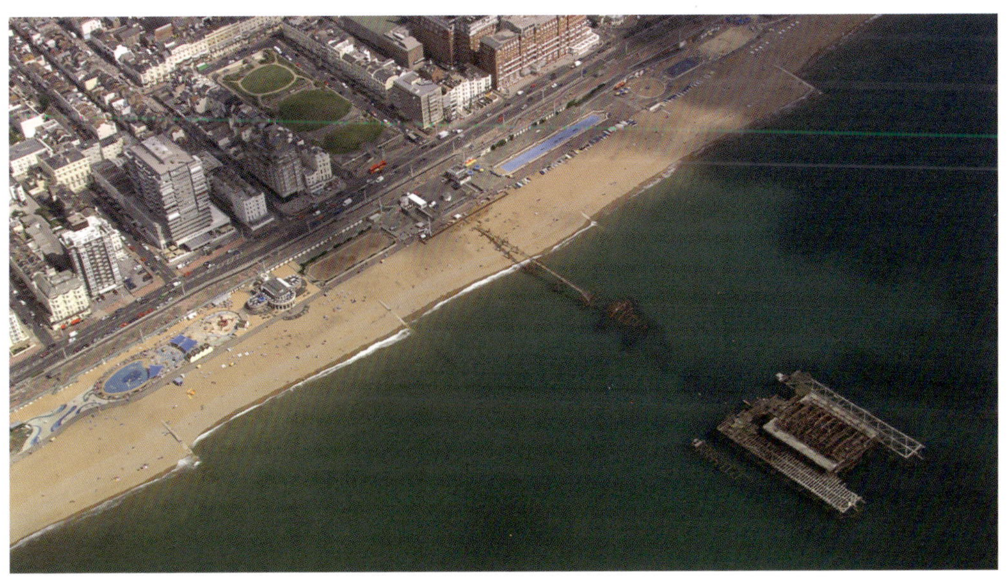

Brighton. The West Pier, opened in 1866, stands opposite Regency Square; it was closed in 1975.

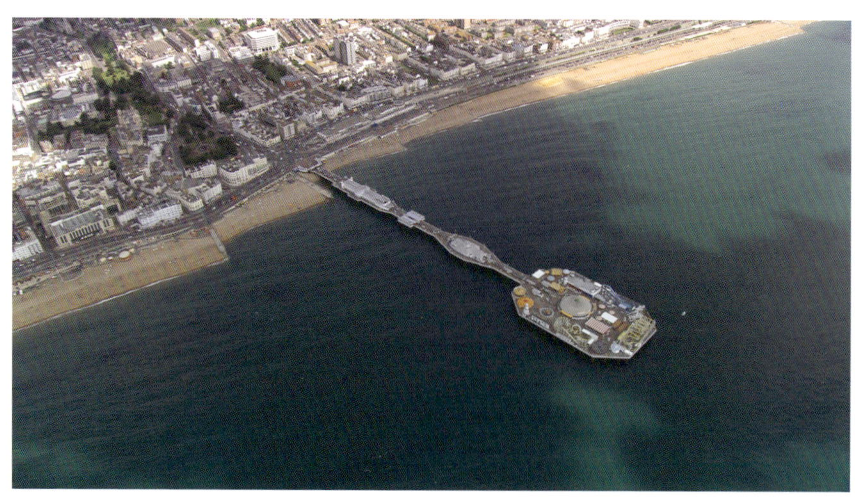

Brighton Pier was opened in 1899 and was known originally as the Palace Pier.

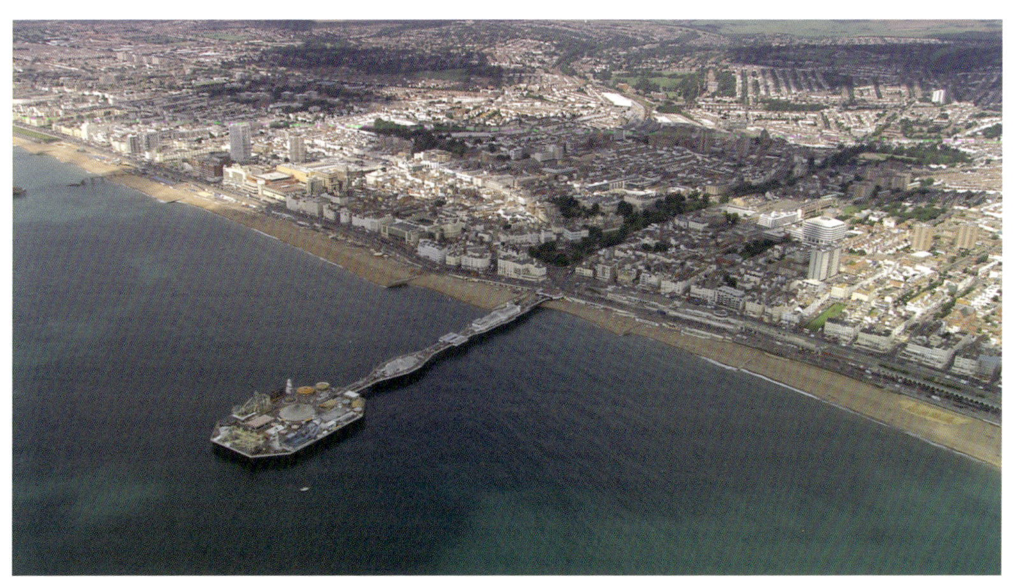

Brighton Pier was once described as the 'grandest pier ever built' and is over 500m long.

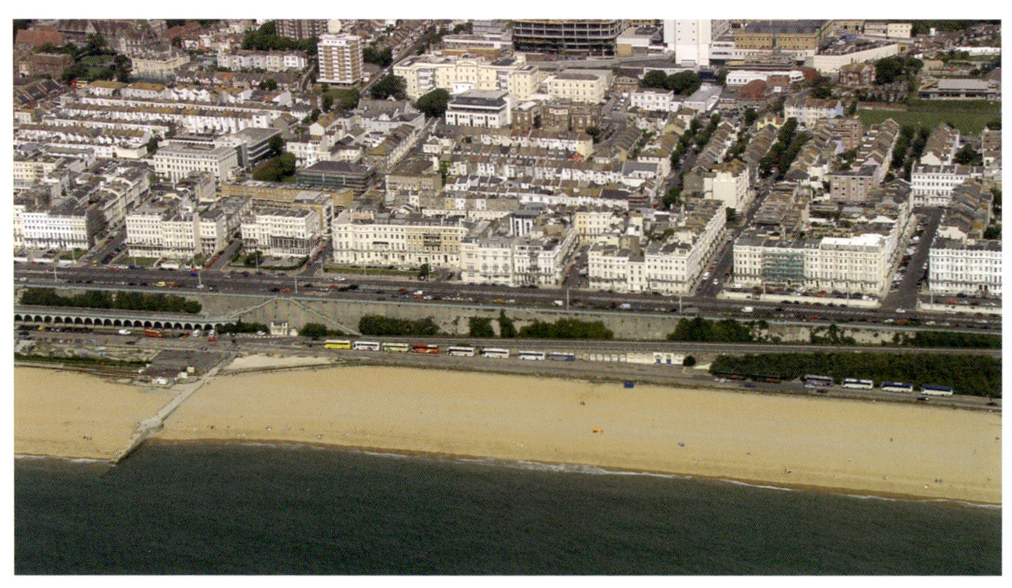

East of Brighton Pier lies Marine Parade with Madeira Drive beneath it, and one of the best beaches in Britain.

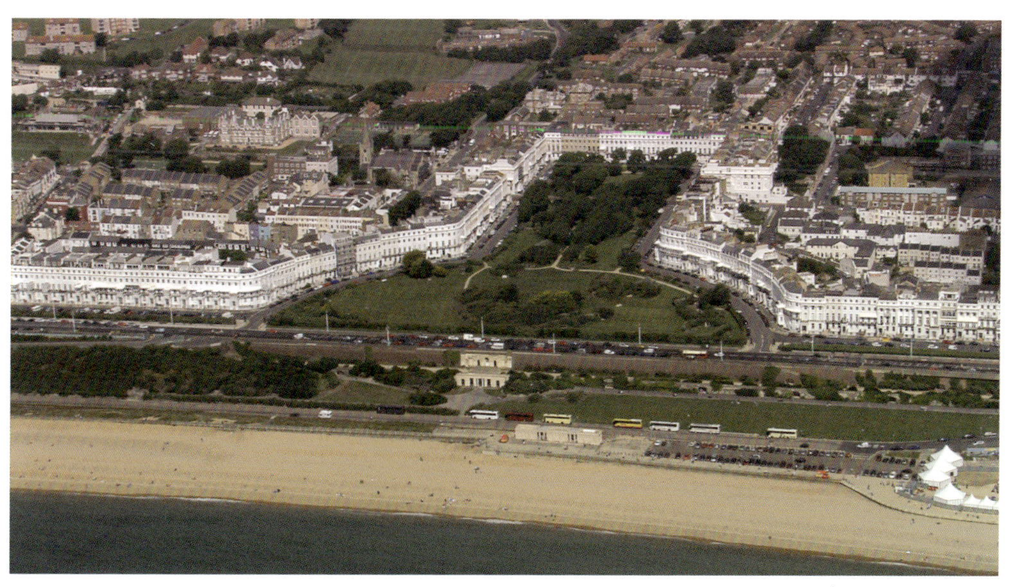

Lewes Crescent and Sussex Square, the grandest of all in the city of Brighton.

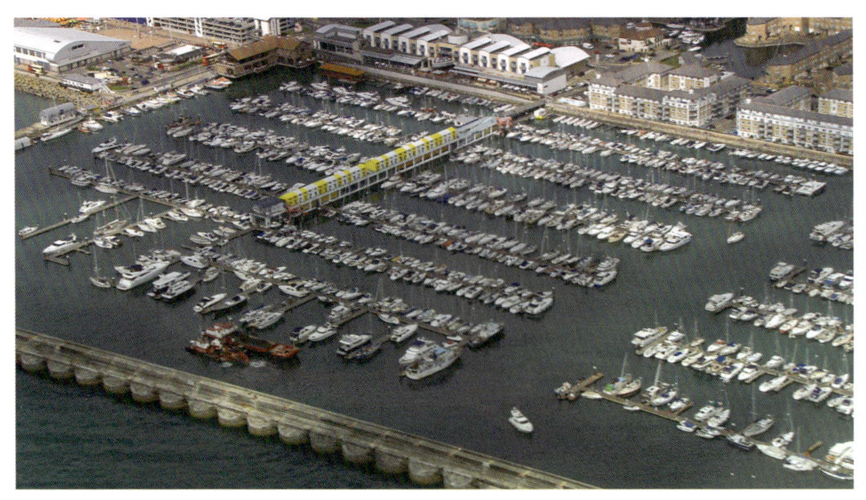

Brighton Marina, not just a yachting harbour but an entertainment and residential centre as well.

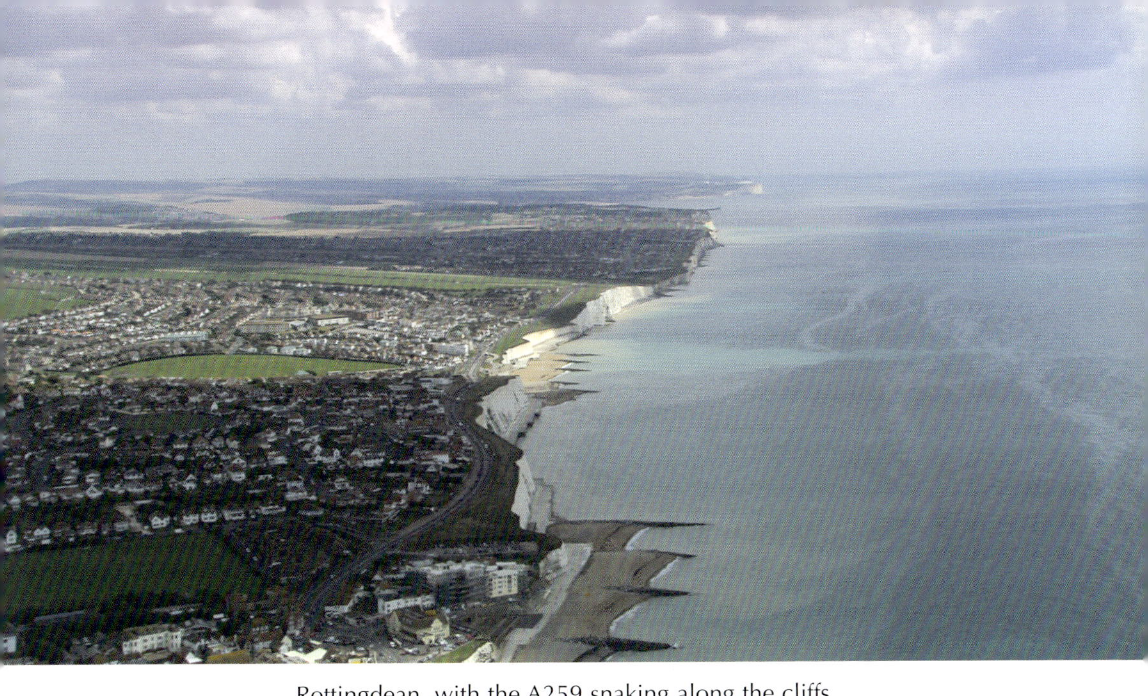

Rottingdean, with the A259 snaking along the cliffs.

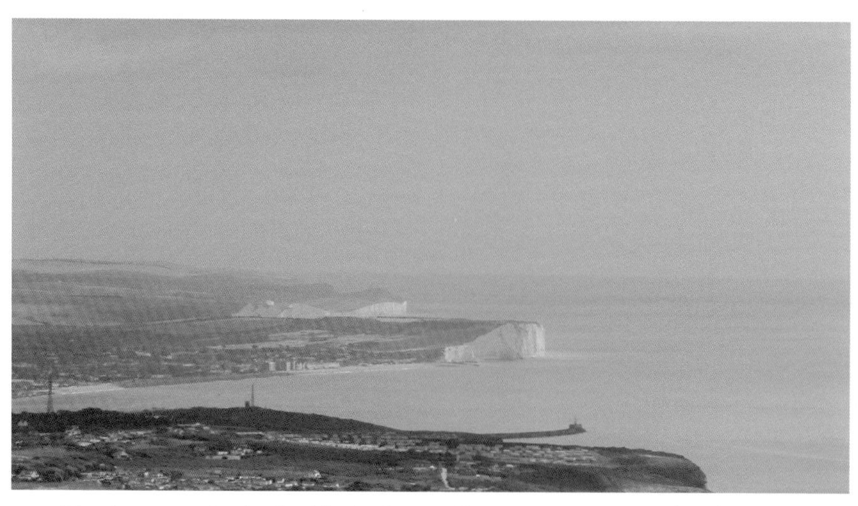

Newhaven to Seaford with the Seven Sisters rearing up in the distance.

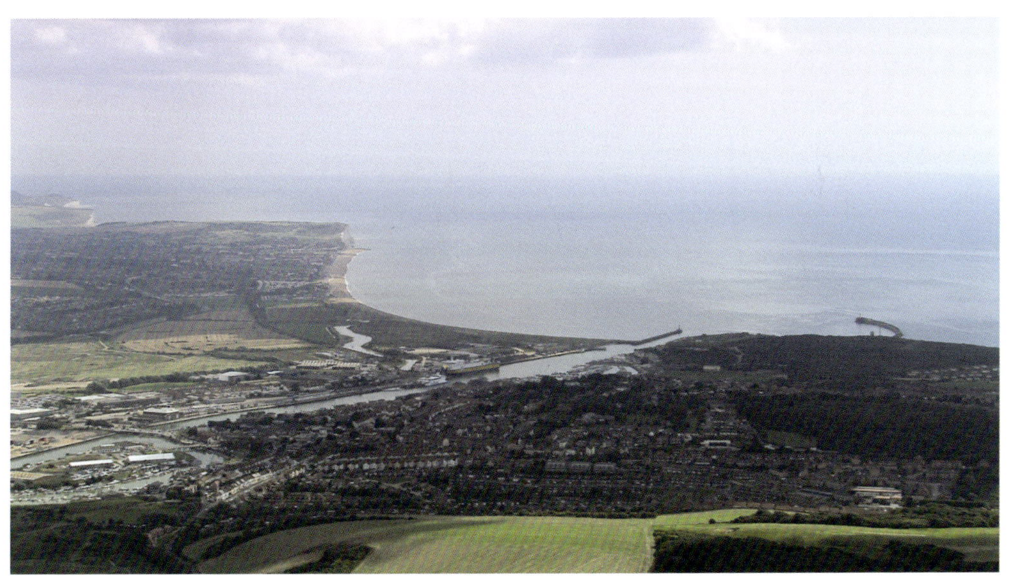

Newhaven remains a busy working port at the mouth of the River Ouse.

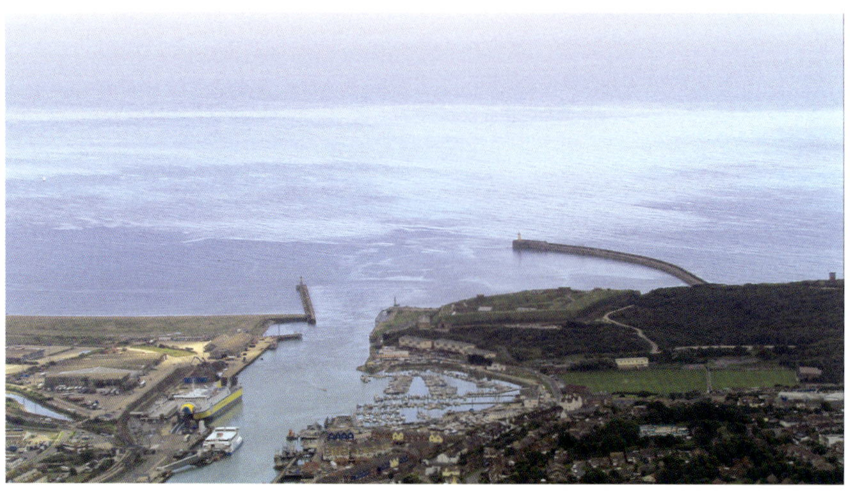

In 1944 troops embarked from Newhaven for D Day landings in Normandy; today you can still cross to Dieppe.

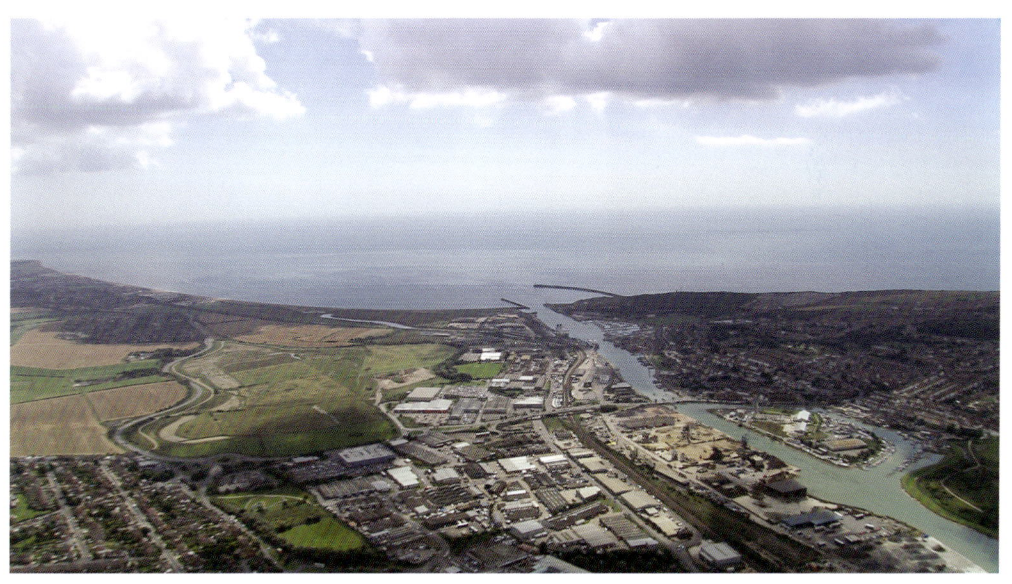

The road bridge in Newhaven can be opened to allow vessels to pass upstream.

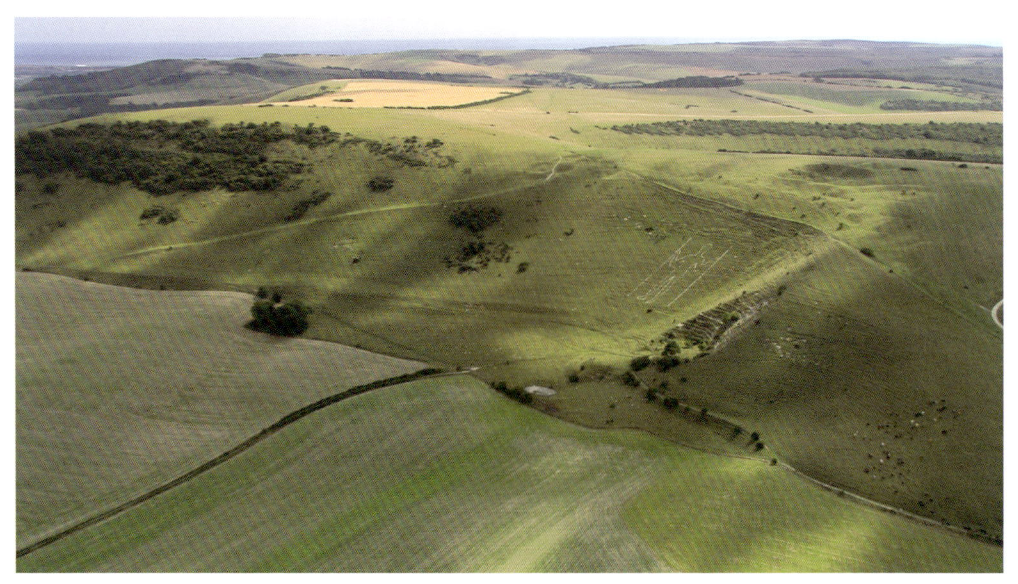

Approaching Windover Hill and the Long Man of Wilmington.

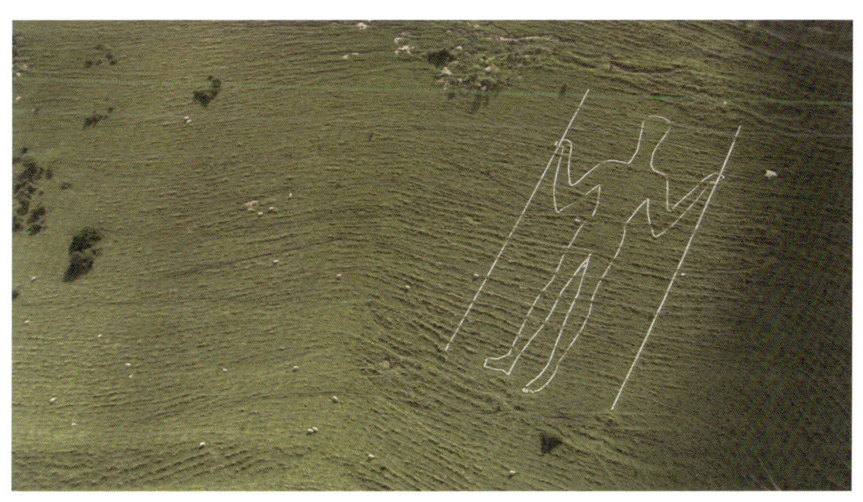

The Long Man of Wilmington at 73m high is perhaps the largest outline of a human figure in Europe.

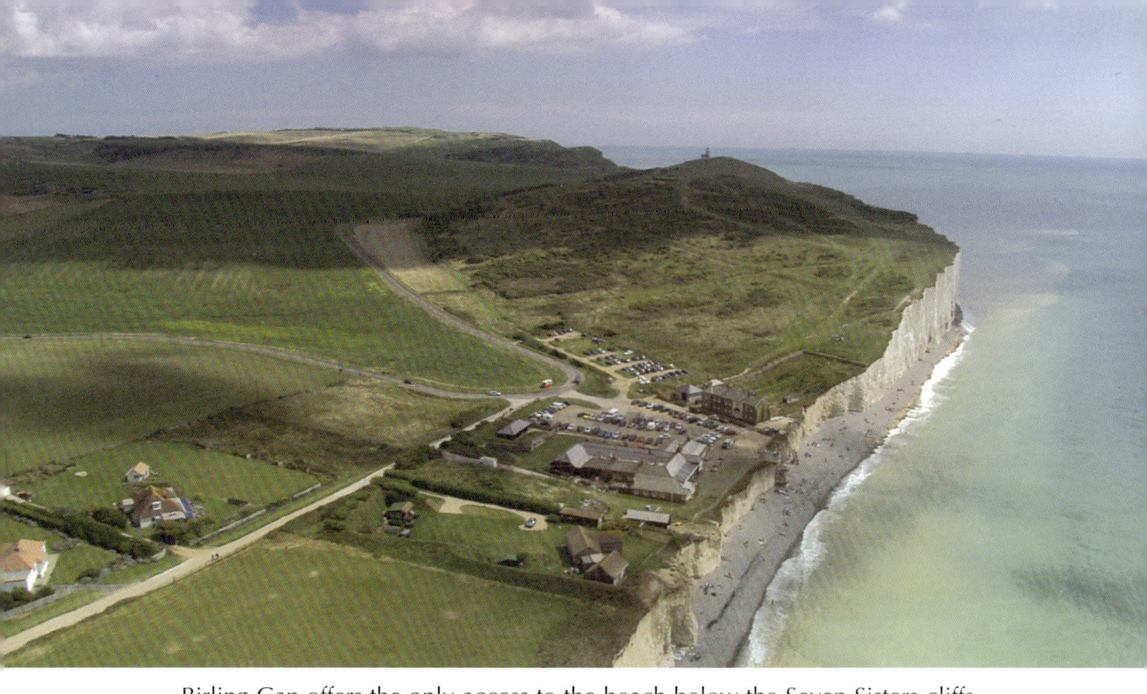

Birling Gap offers the only access to the beach below the Seven Sisters cliffs.

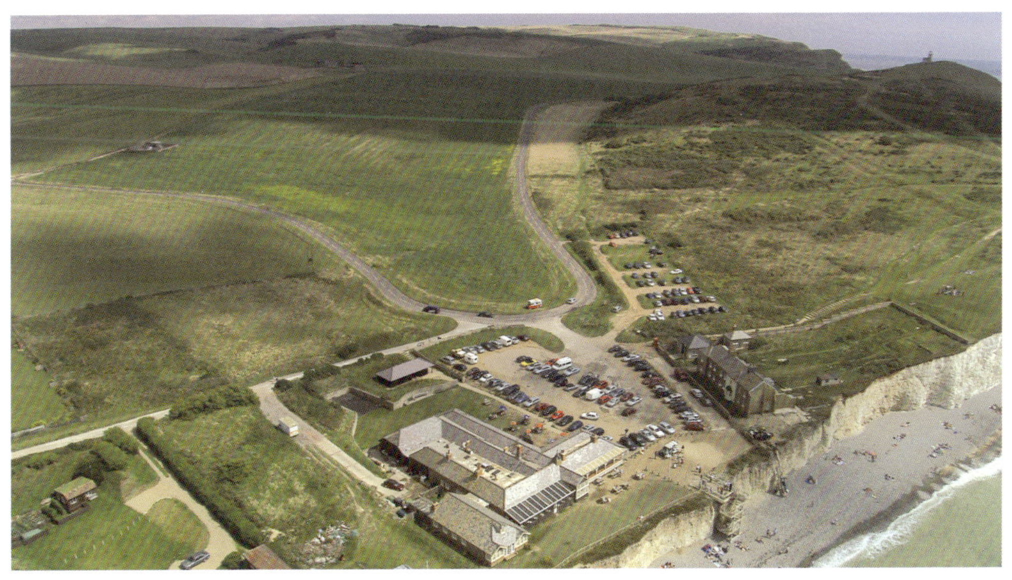

At Birling Gap the receding cliffs threaten the houses and hotel.

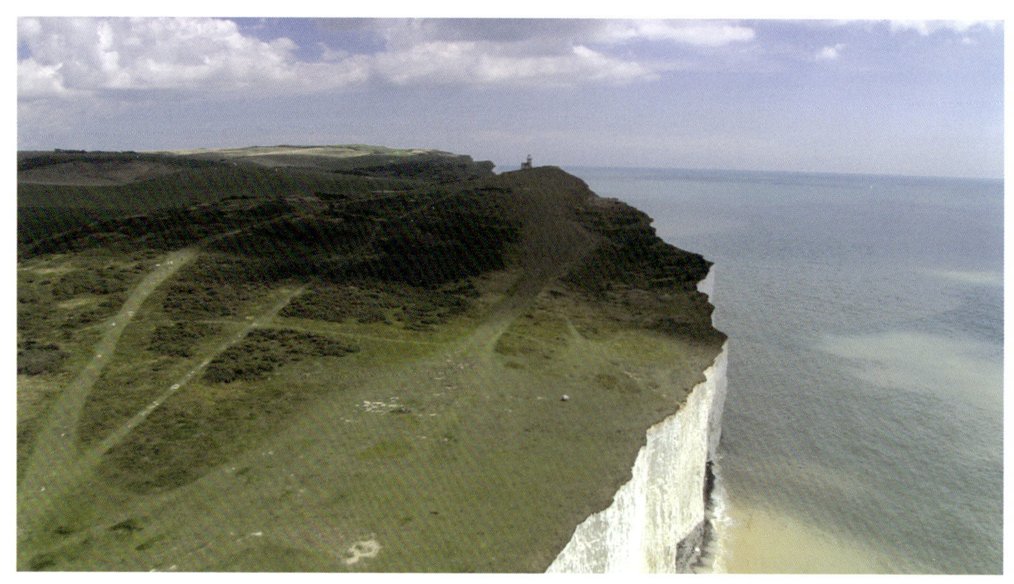

Beachy Head, approaching the Belle Tout lighthouse.

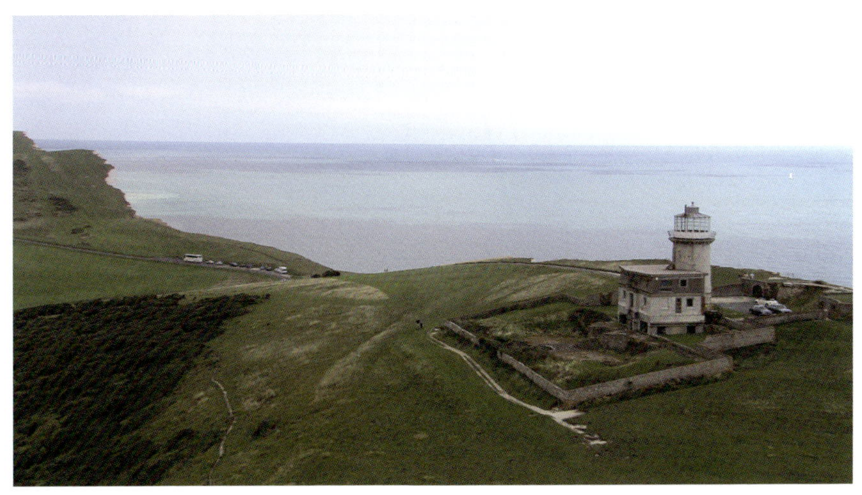

Now a private house, Belle Tout lighthouse was moved inland by 50ft in 1999 after the cliff edge came dangerously close.

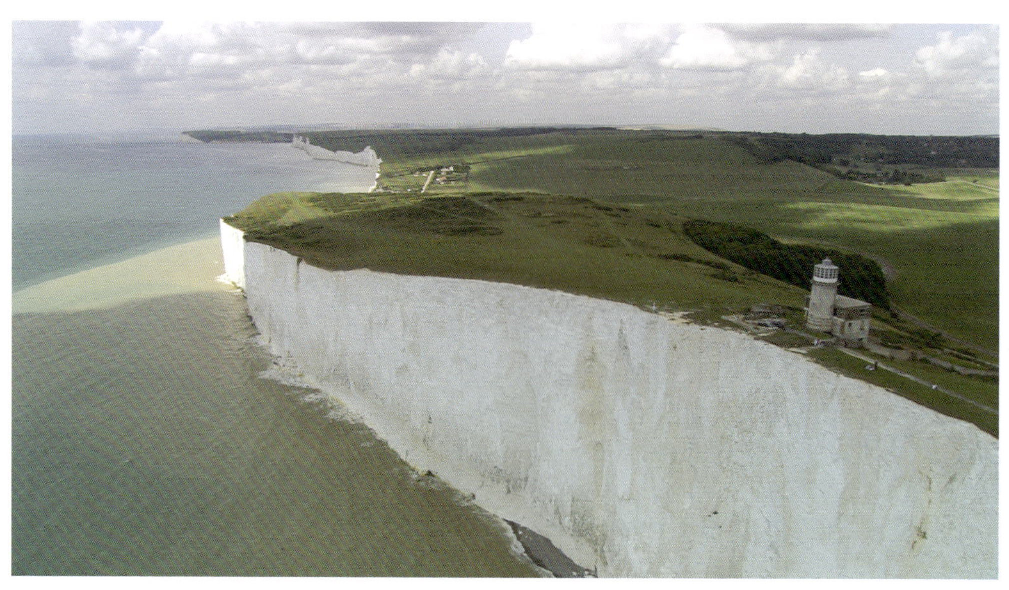

The Seven Sisters chalk cliffs stretch for nearly 8km westwards from Beachy Head.

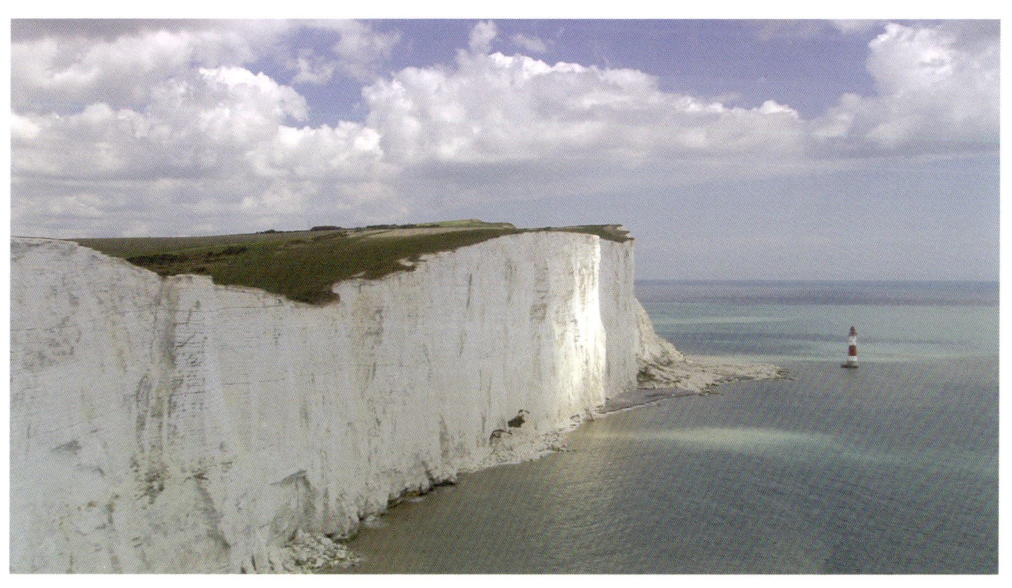

The Seven Sisters are among the most unspoiled coastal areas in Britain and certainly the most dramatic.

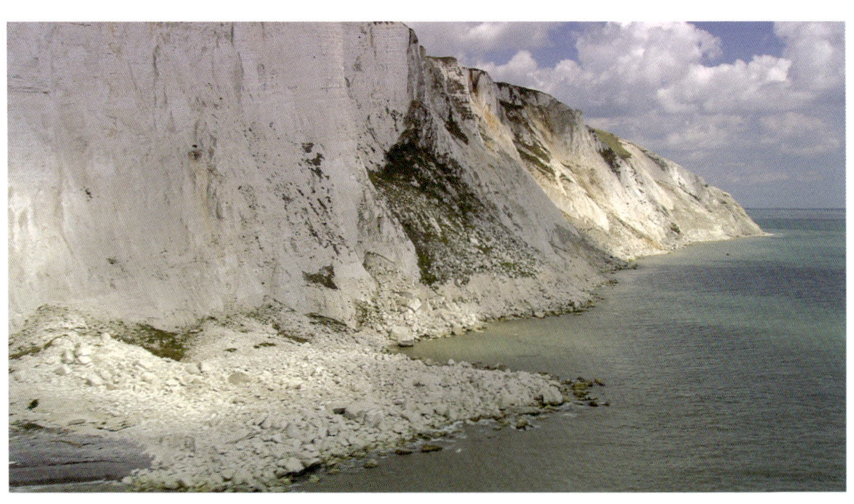

Cliff falls are common, particularly after freezing conditions.

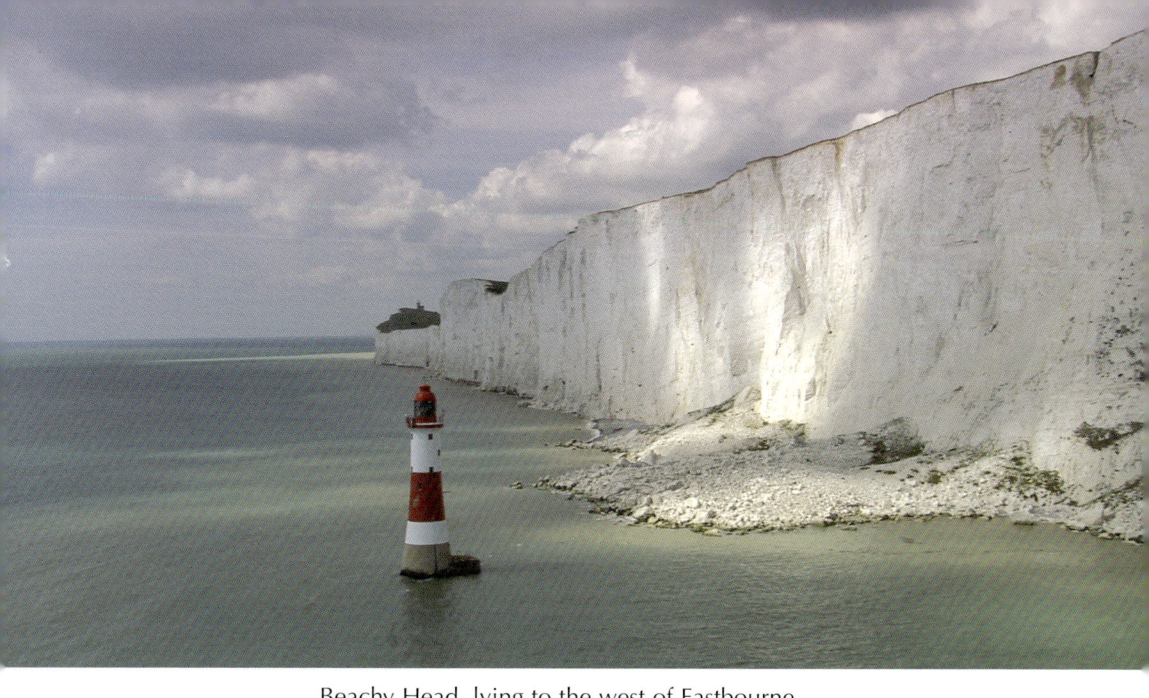

Beachy Head, lying to the west of Eastbourne.

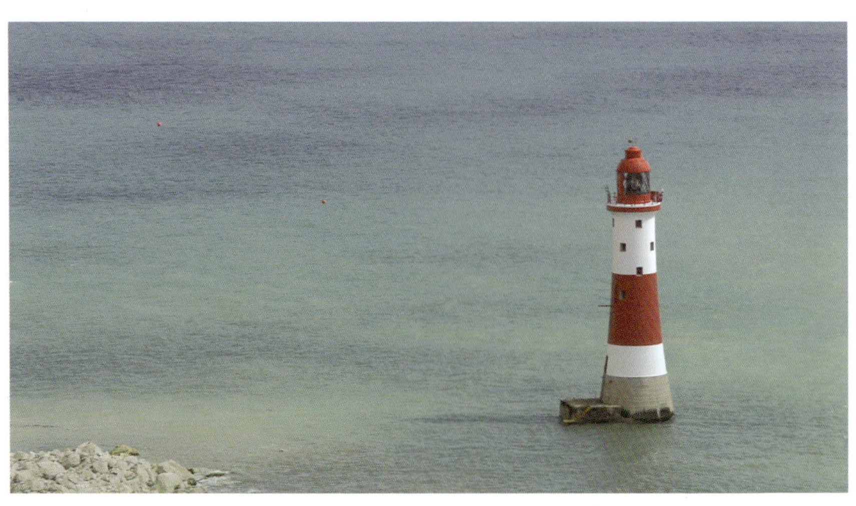

The red and white lighthouse at Beachy Head was built in 1902,
the materials lowered by aerial ropeway.

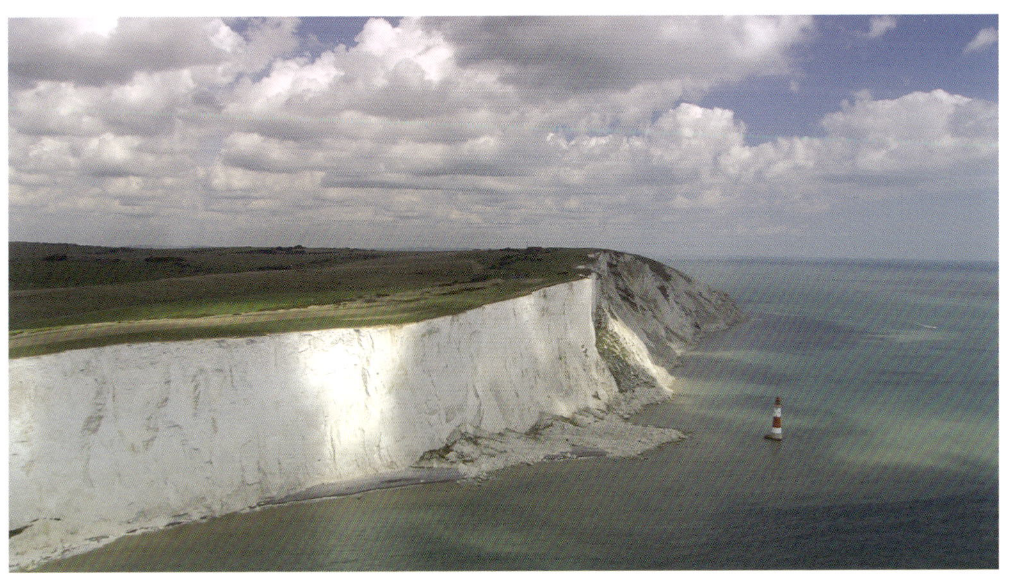

The cliffs at Beachy Head at 163m are the highest chalk cliffs on the South Coast.

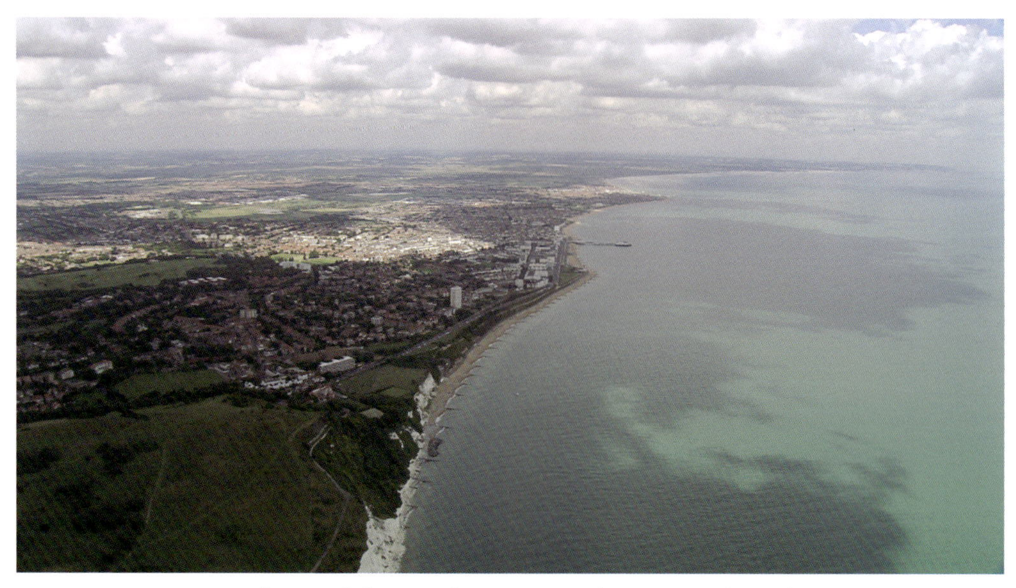

From Beachy Head the coastline turns northeast towards Eastbourne.

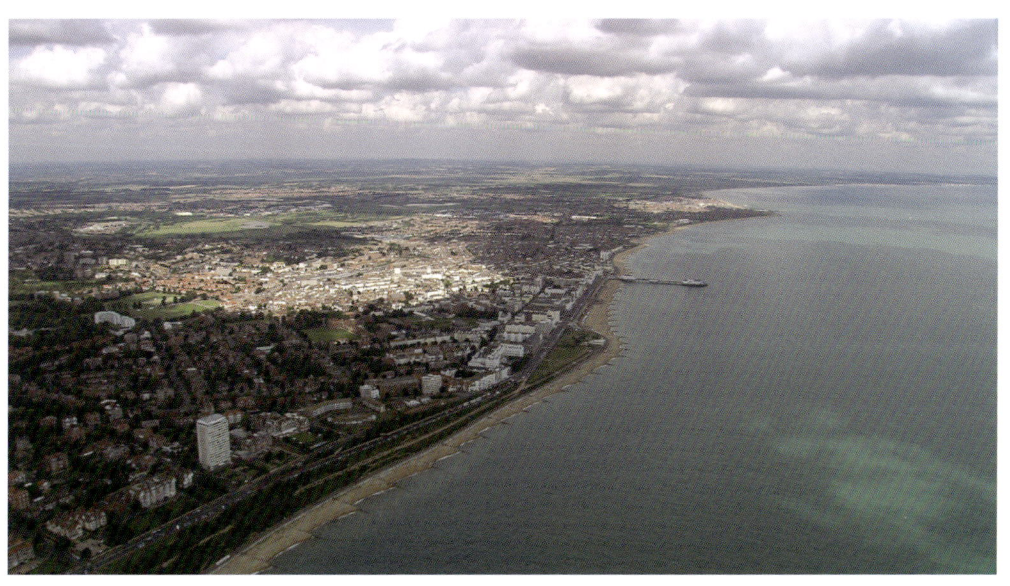

Eastbourne was developed as a resort by the Dukes of Devonshire, and their influence is recorded in street and hotel names.

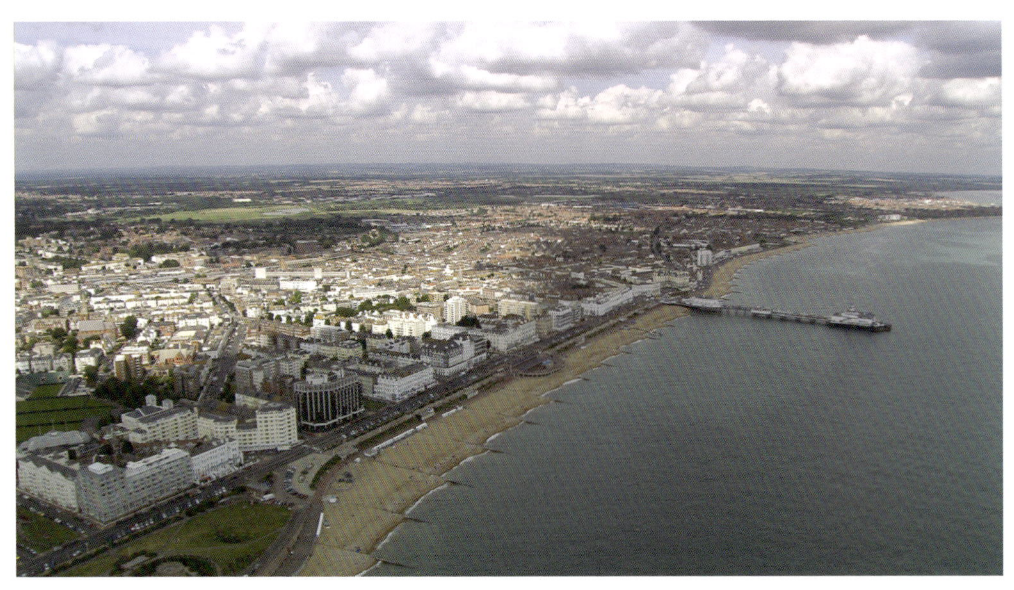

Eastbourne's famous Devonshire Park international tennis centre is seen on the left of this view over the town.

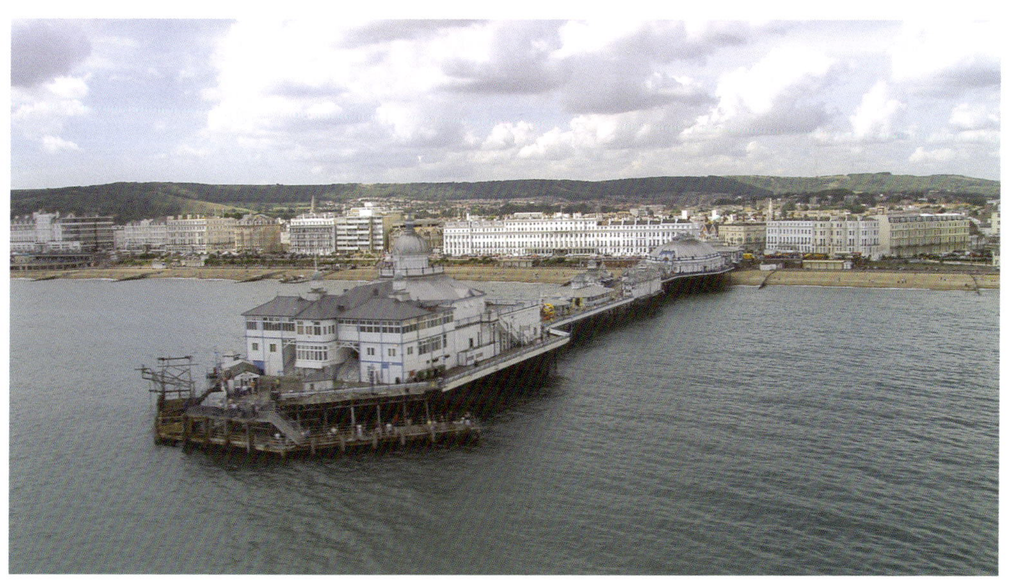

The Victorian pier at Eastbourne was designed by Eugenius Birch and opened in 1872.

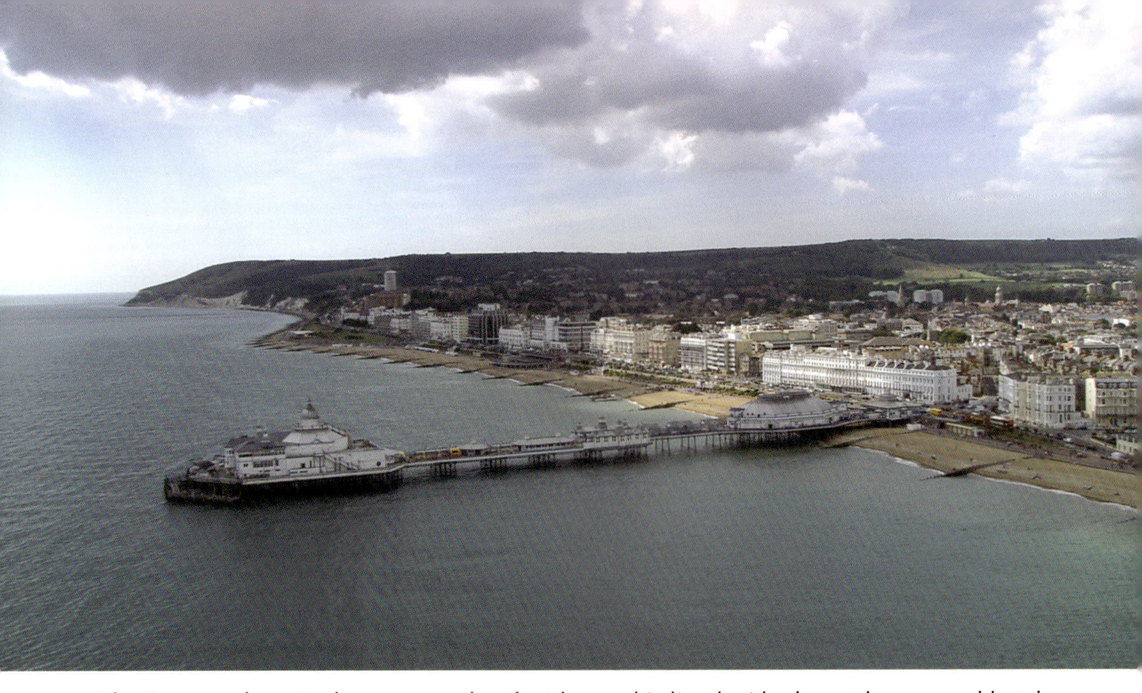

The Promenade at Eastbourne stretches for 5km and is lined with elegant houses and hotels.

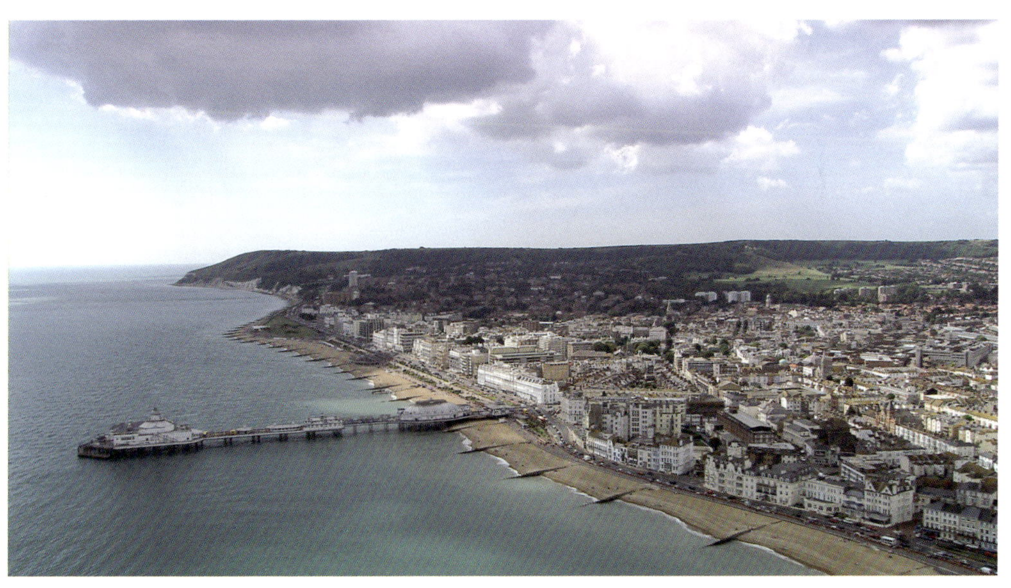

Eastbourne is known as the 'Empress of the watering places' but is also the gateway to glorious countryside and the start of the South Downs Way.

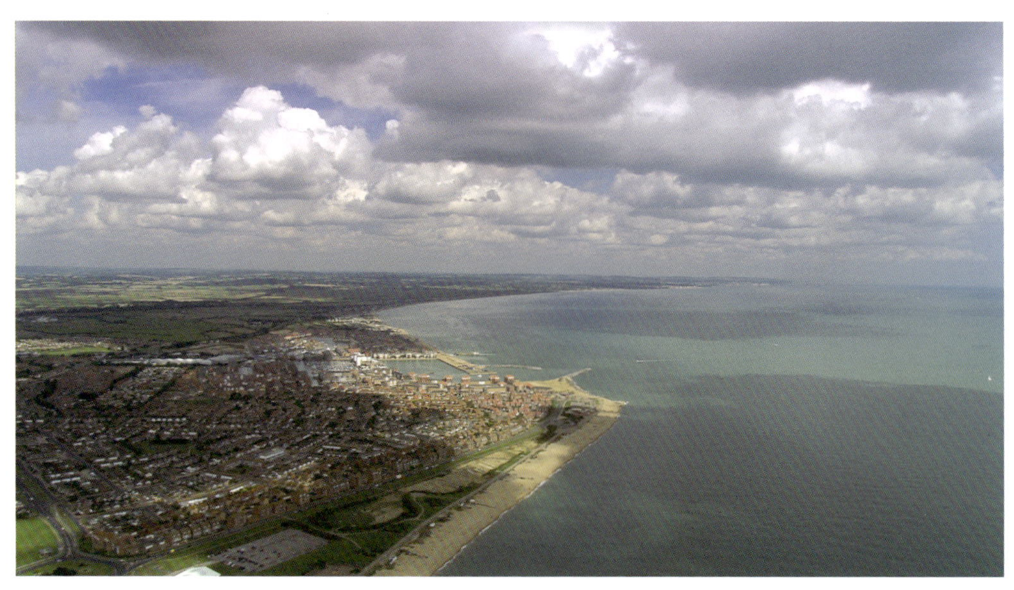

Eastbourne's Sovereign Harbour marina lies on the eastern edge of the town.

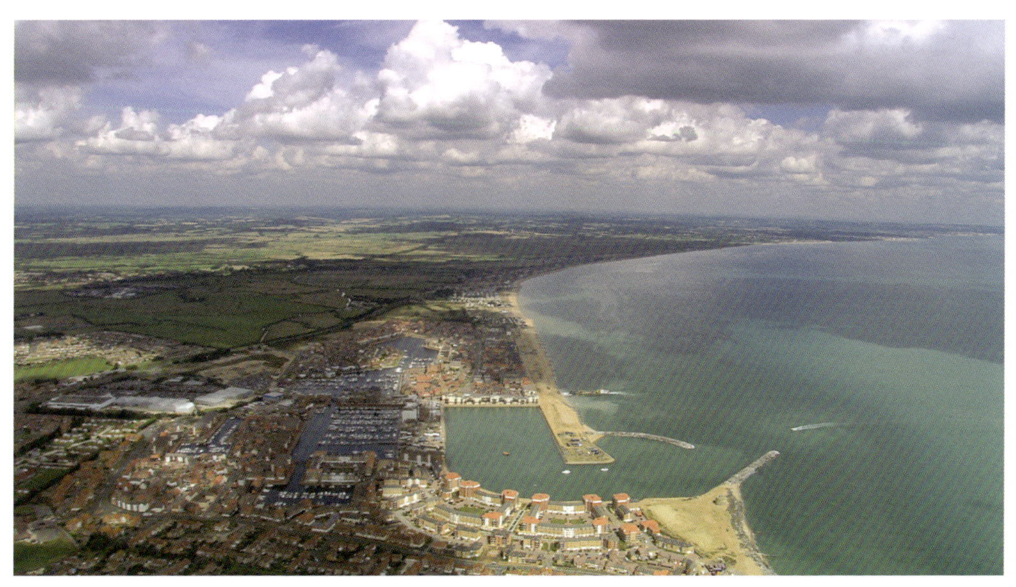

The exclusive Sovereign Harbour was opened in 1993 and consists of five separate mooring basins.

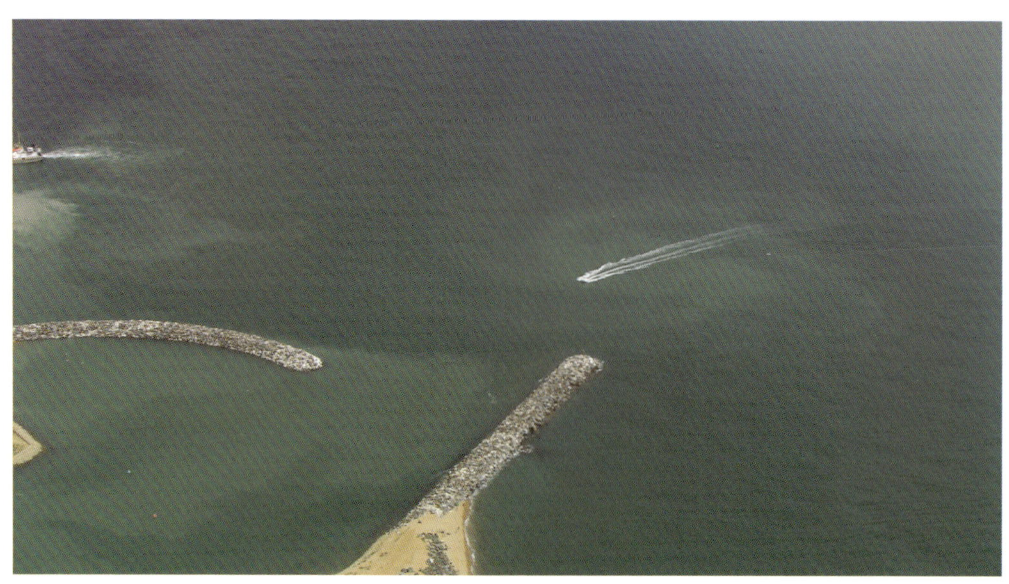

The entrance to Eastbourne's marina, with its protective mole.

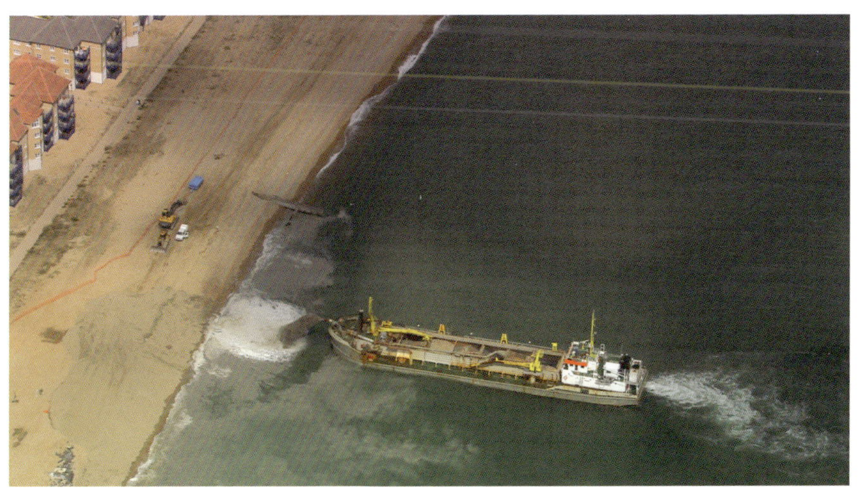

A dredger lies outside the Eastbourne marina complex.

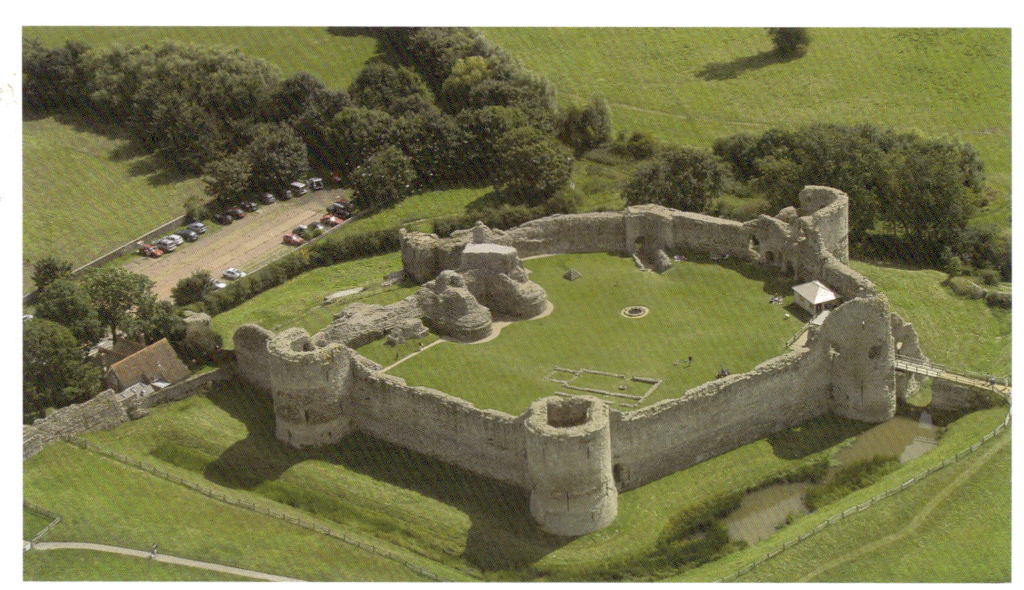

Pevensey Castle was originally built by the Romans, and two-thirds of their towered walls still stand.

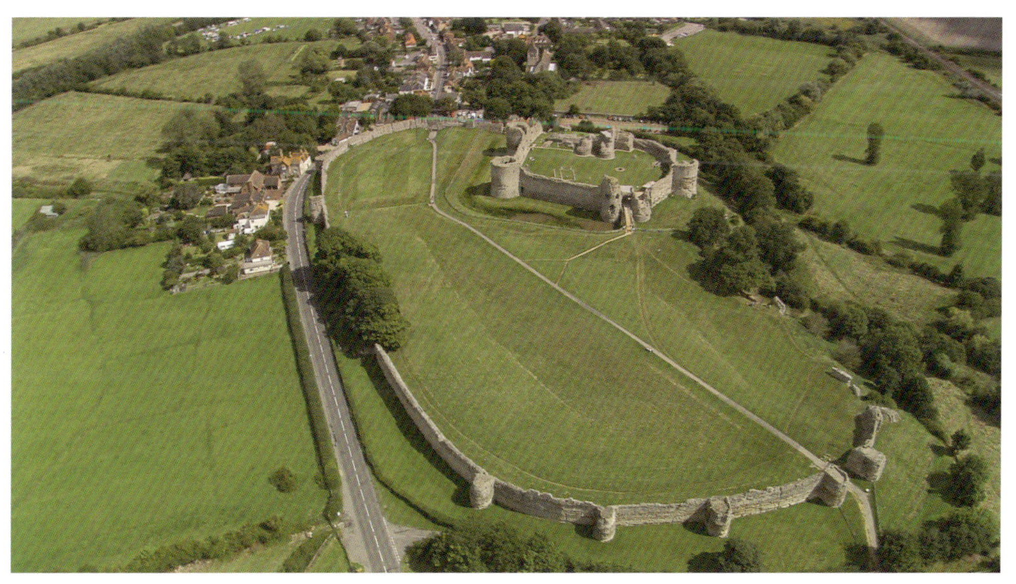

After the conquest, Pevensey was turned into a Norman Castle with a stone keep and bailey.

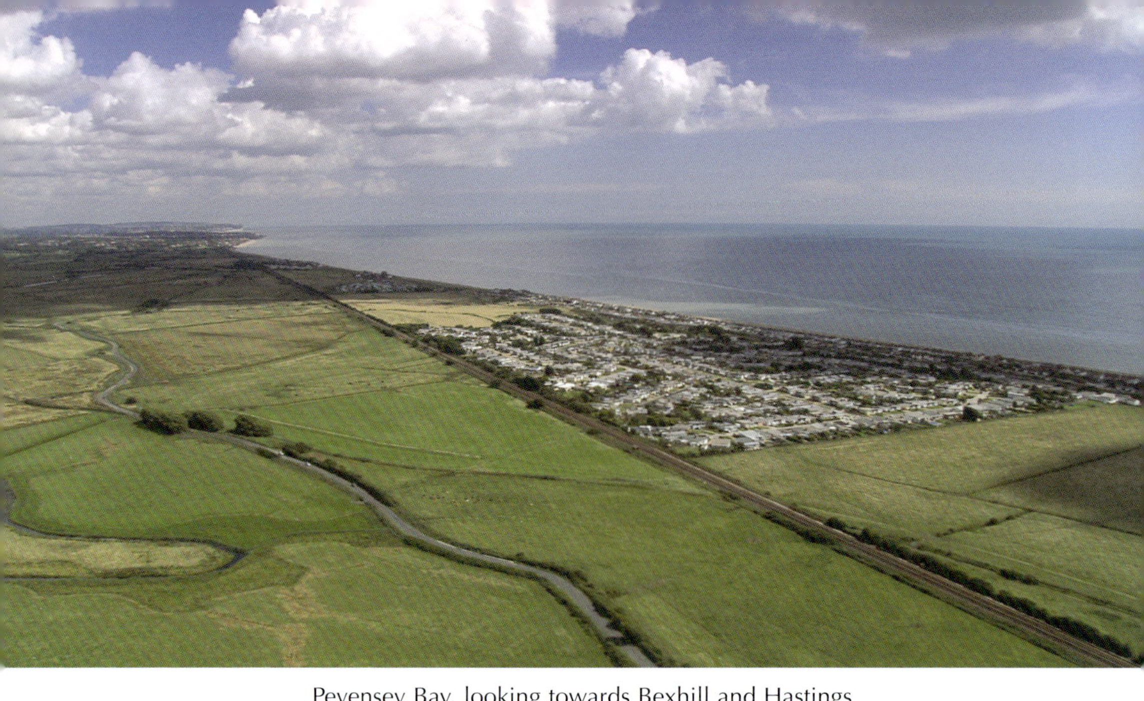

Pevensey Bay, looking towards Bexhill and Hastings

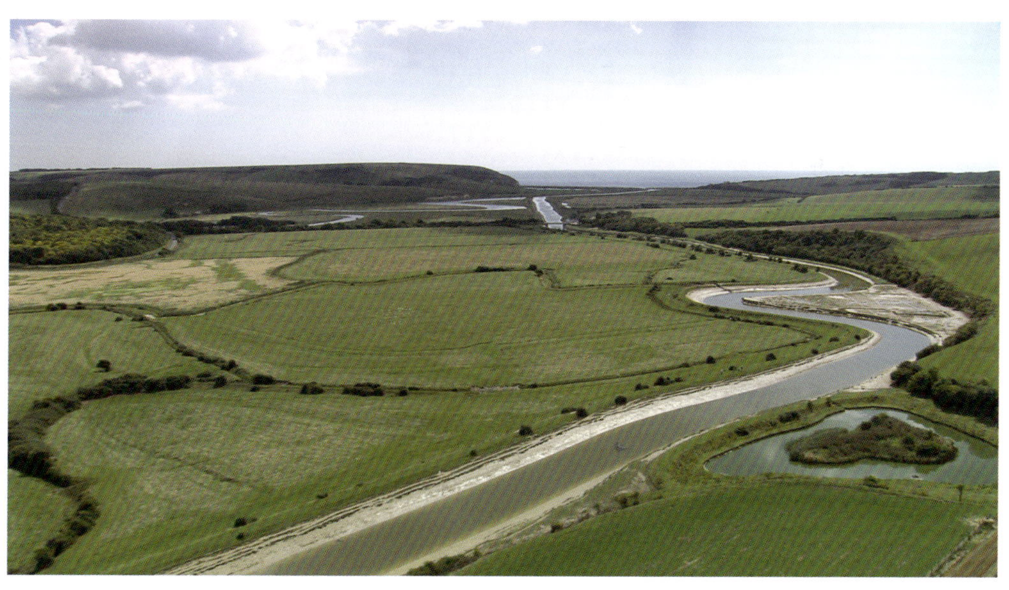

The River Cuckmere meanders its way to the coast.

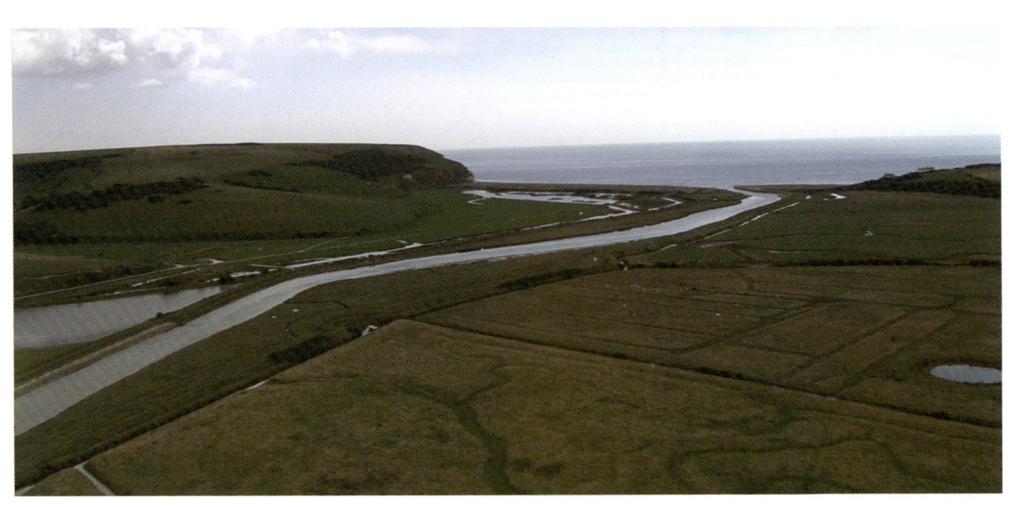

The River Cuckmere enters the English Channel at Cuckmere Haven, part of the Seven Sisters Country Park.

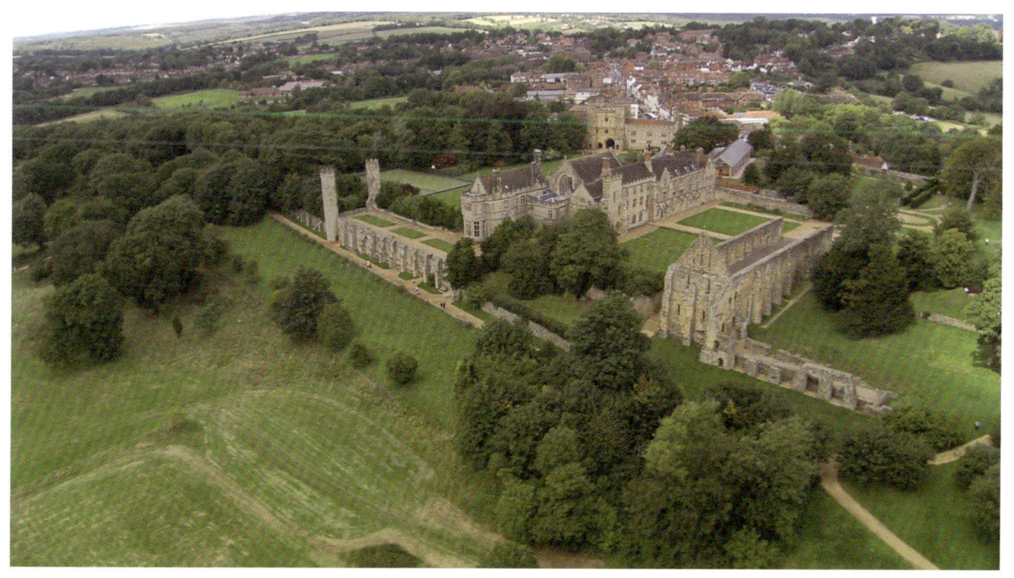

Battle Abbey was founded by William the Conqueror to commemorate his victory in 1066.

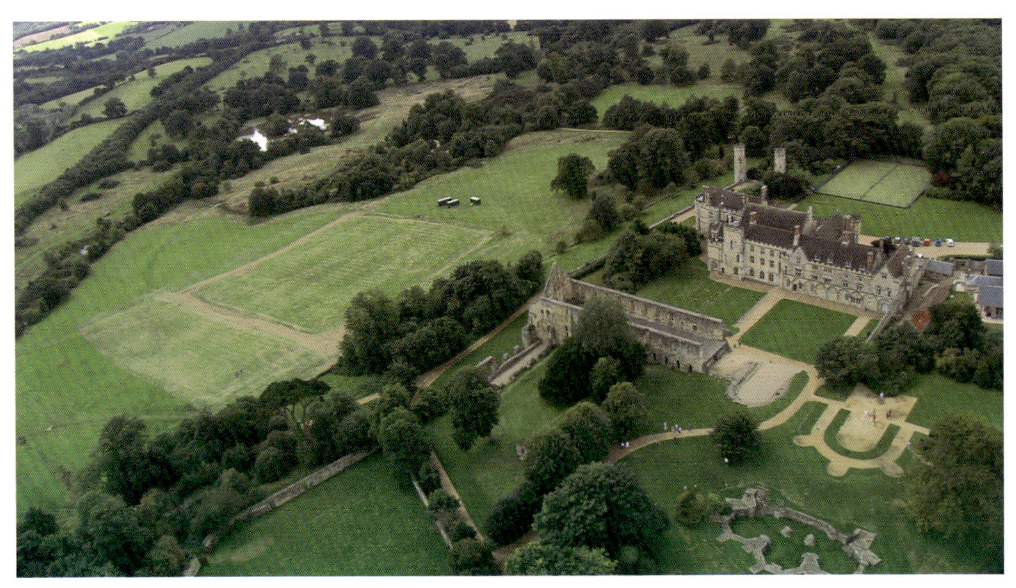

Although the famous battle is termed 'of Hastings', it actually took place here, some 7 miles away, then called Senlac.

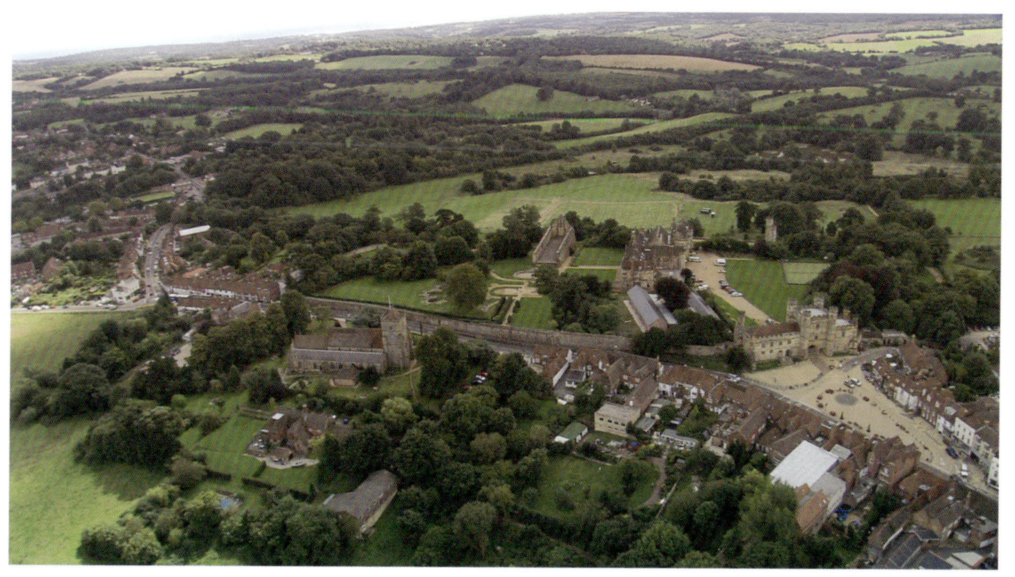

King Harold of England fell on the spot where the Abbey's high altar stands.

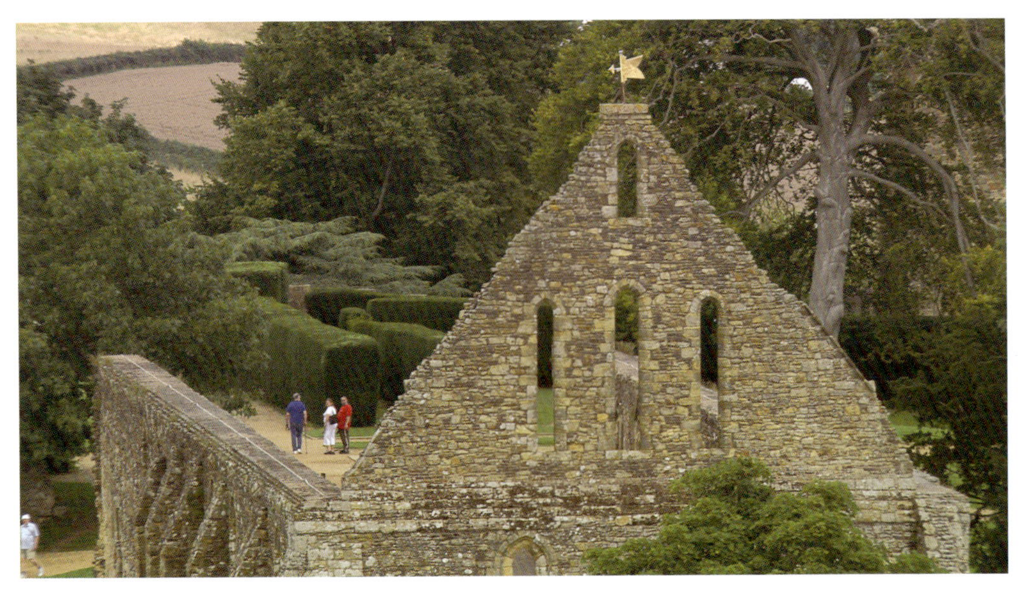

Battle Abbey was largely destroyed in the Dissolution of the Monasteries.

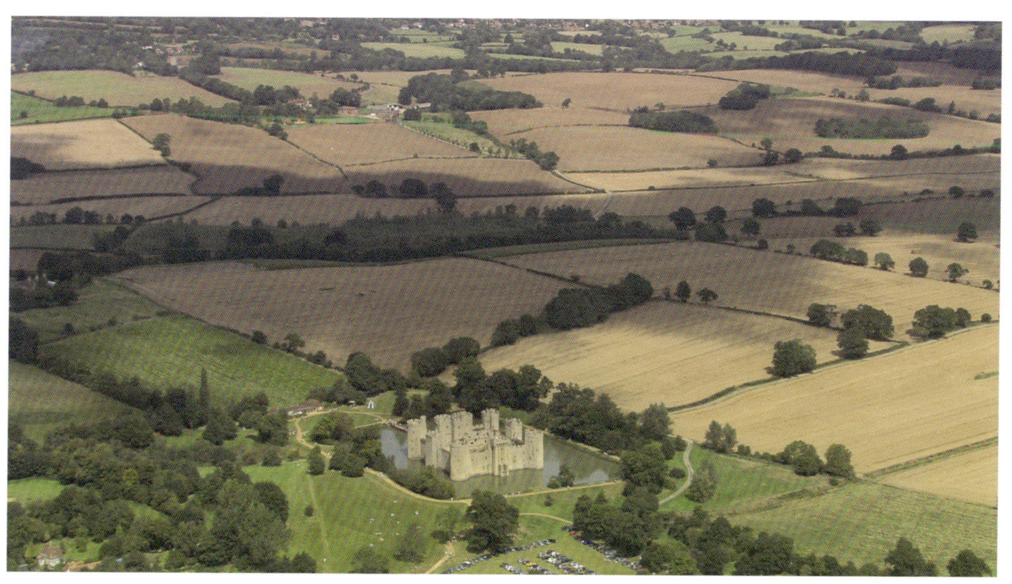

Bodiam Castle lies in the wide valley of the River Rother and was designed to be a defense against the French in the 1300s.

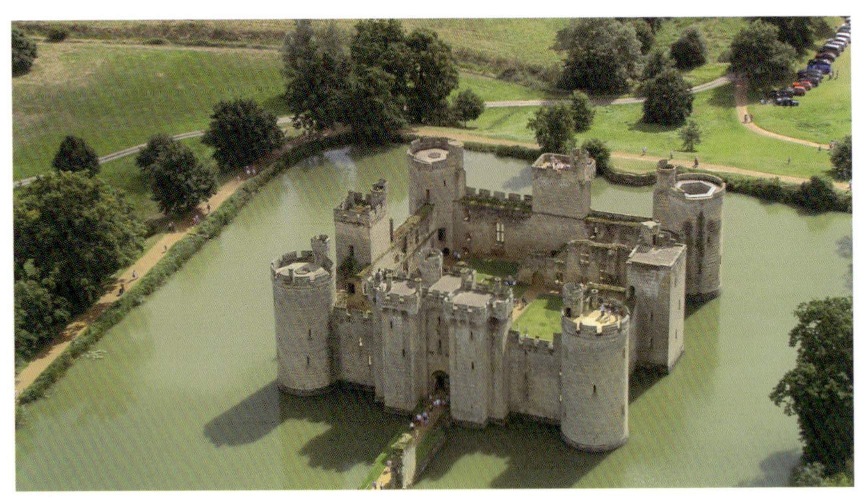

Bodiam's moat may have been as much for show as defense, but certainly gives it a 'fairytale' appearance.

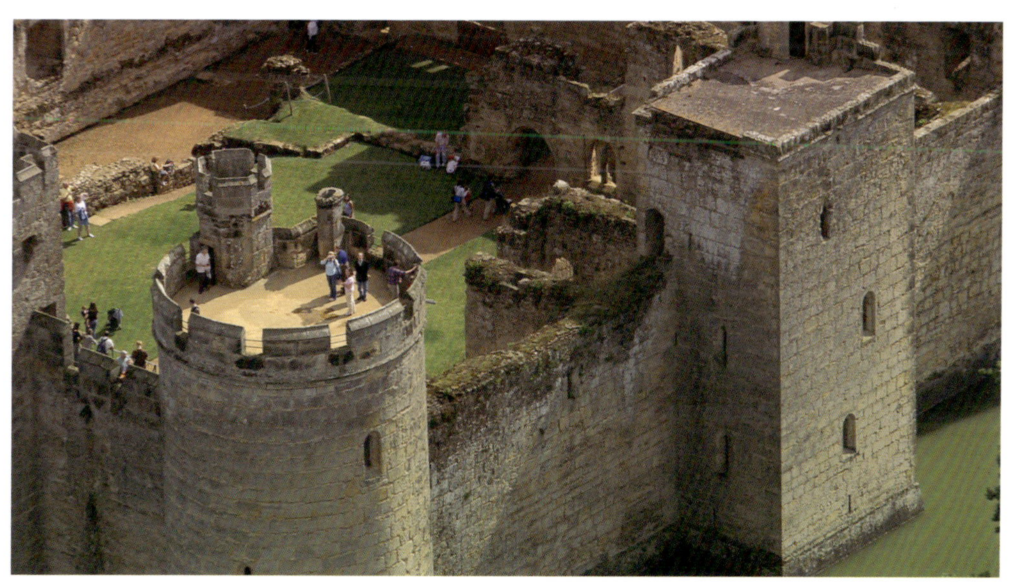

Much of Bodiam Castle was dismantled in the Civil War but it is still possible to climb to the battlements.

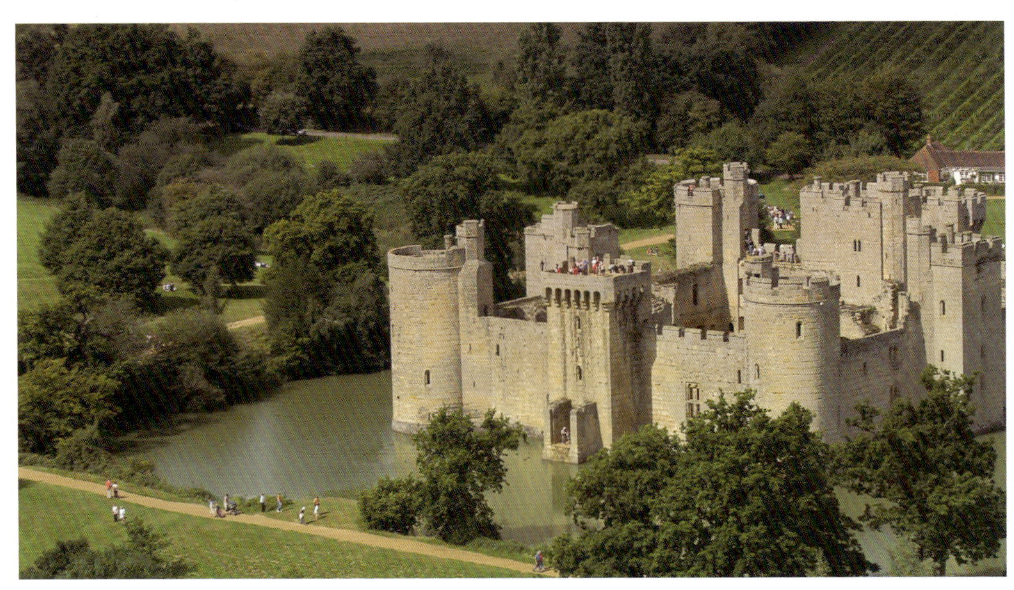

Bodiam was rescued from ruin in the nineteenth century and was given to the National Trust by Lord Curzon in 1925.

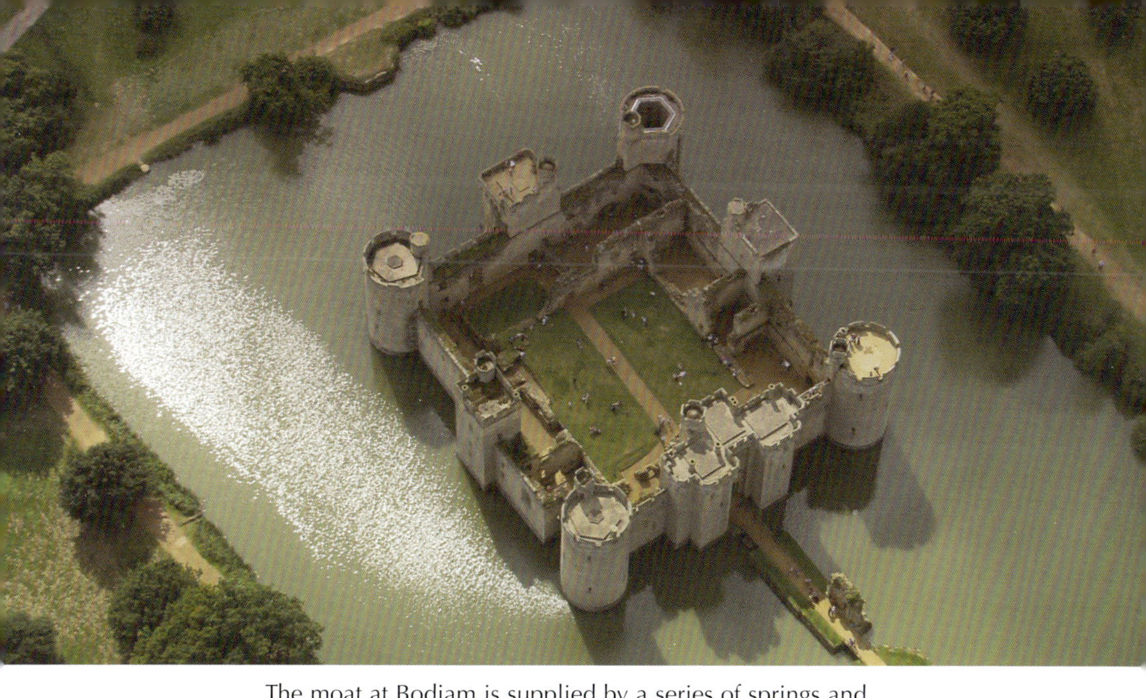

The moat at Bodiam is supplied by a series of springs and lies some way above the level of the nearby river.

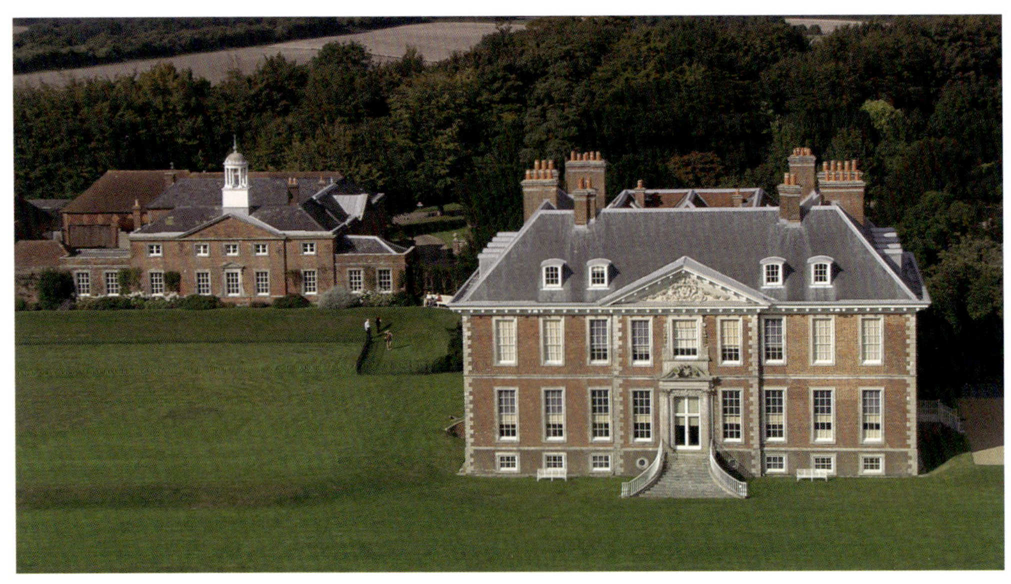

Uppark House, in a commanding position on the South Downs, was built around 1690 for Lord Grey.

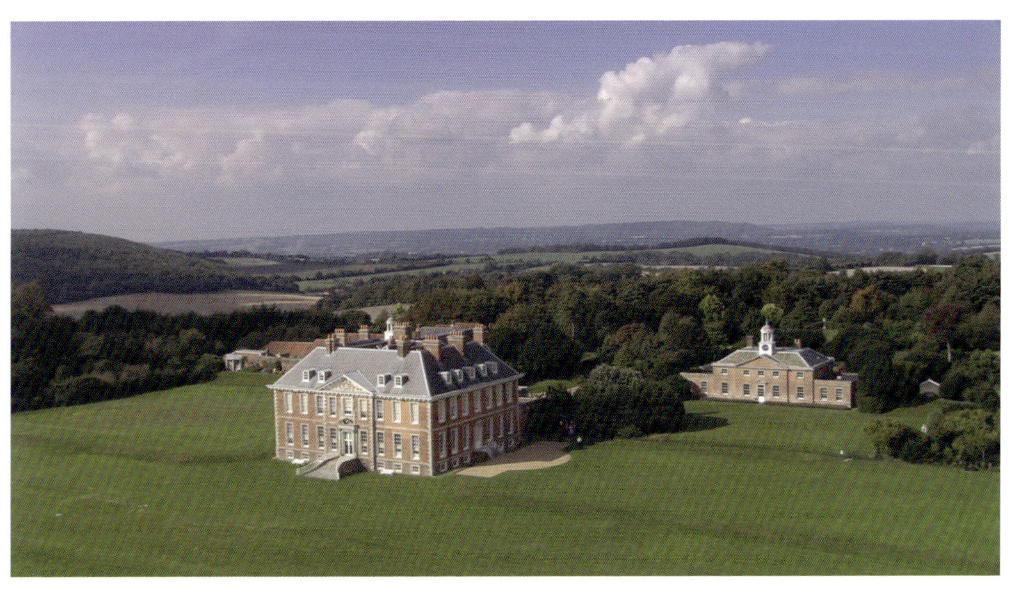

Uppark was given to the National Trust in 1954 and was regarded as a jewel because of its carefully-preserved original decoration.

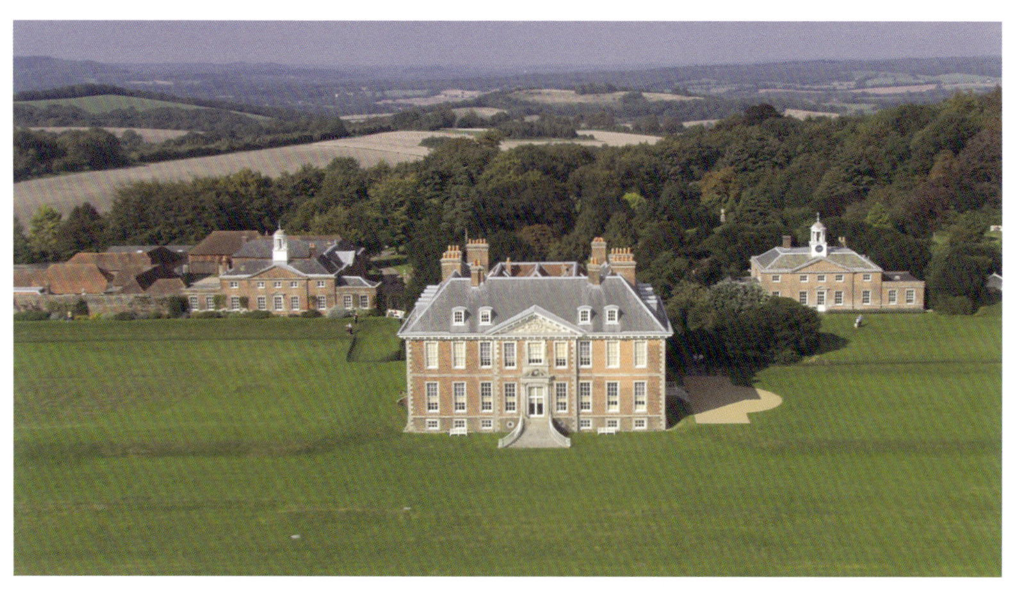

In 1989 a fire severely damaged Uppark's State Rooms.
However, the house was completely restored and re-opened in 1995.

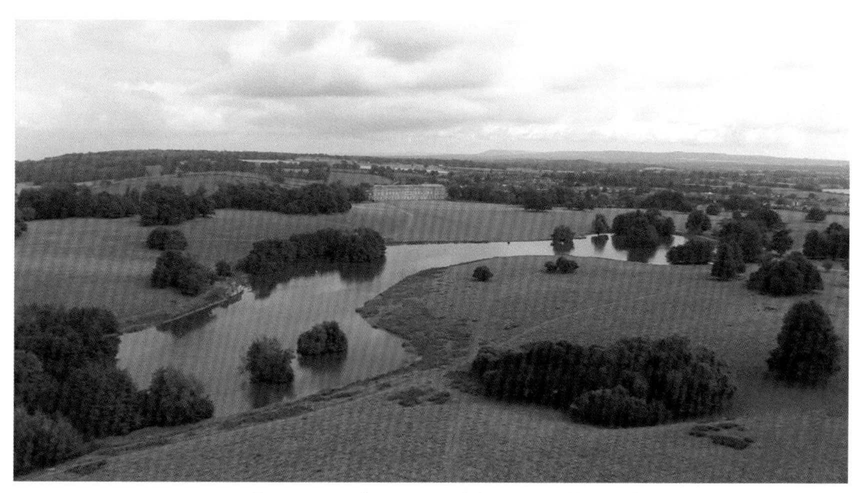

Petworth House, the seat of the Wyndham family
was given to the National Trust in 1947.

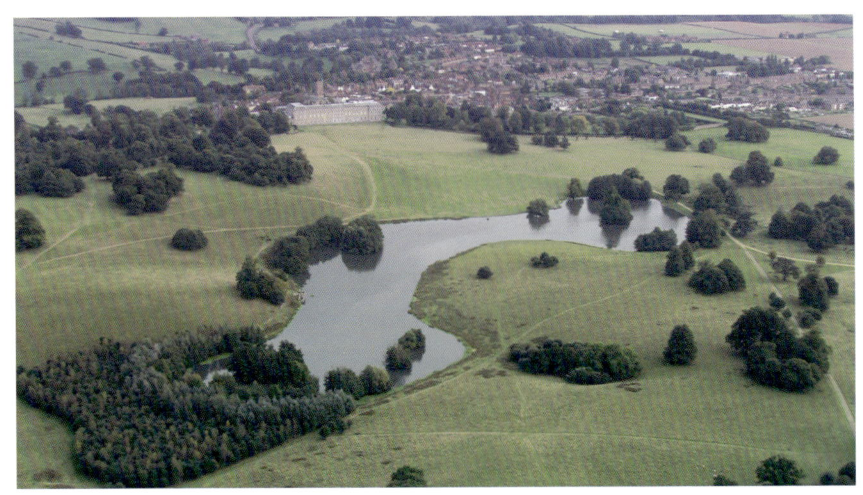

The present mansion at Petworth was built between 1688 and 1696 on a palatial scale.

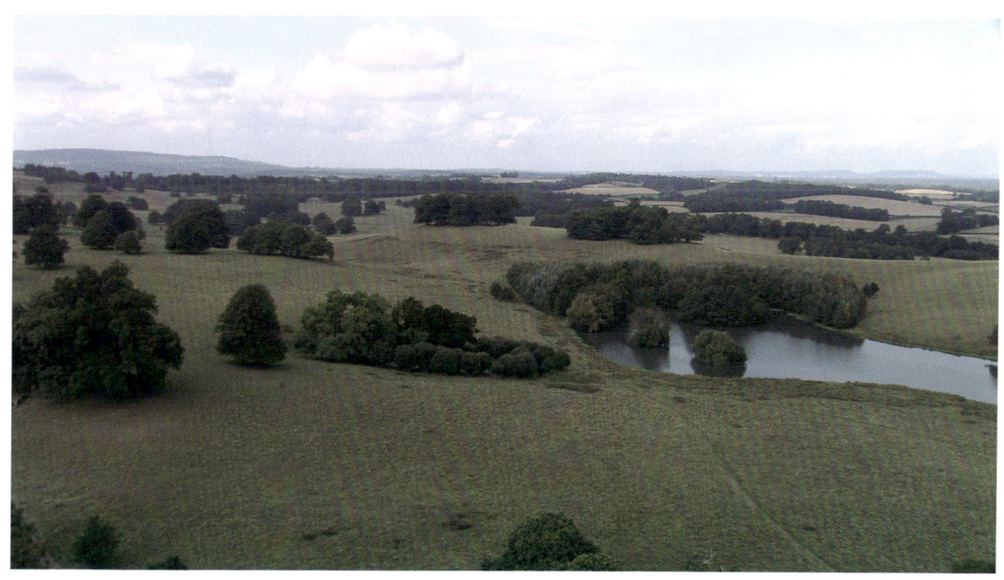

The park at Petworth was laid out by Capability Brown and was a particular inspiration to the artist Turner.

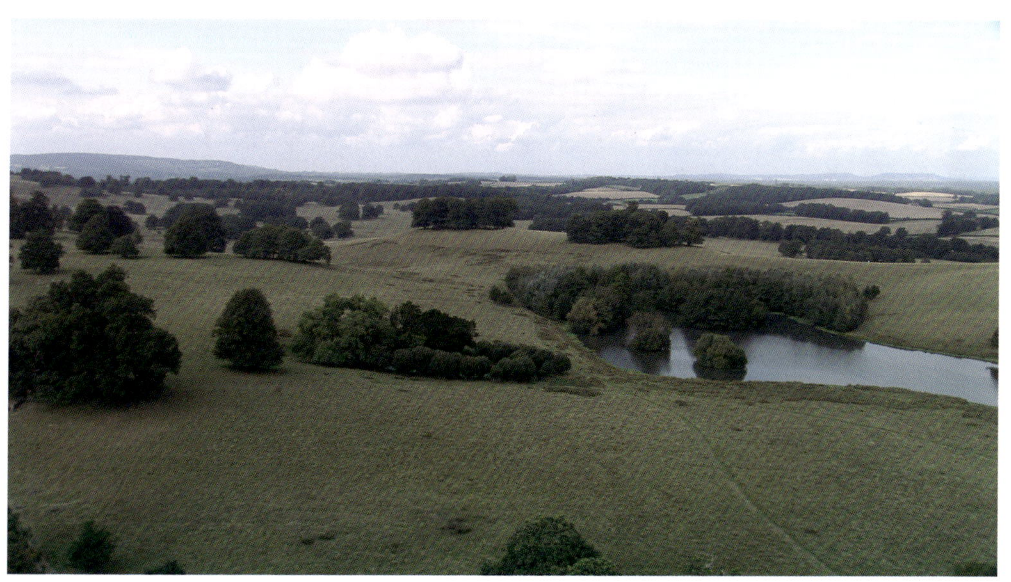

The park at Petworth was laid out by Capability Brown and was a particular inspiration to the artist Turner.

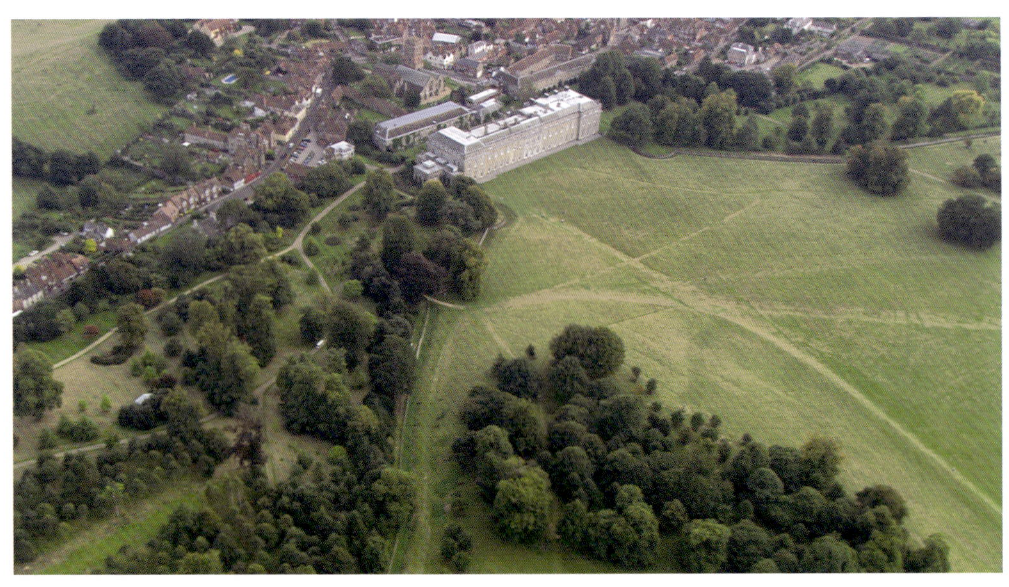

The long west front of Petworth House dominates the village that lies behind it.